"In a forceful, fast-paced, and well-informed narrative, Marc Favreau lets readers experience—no, live!—the worst economic collapse in US history....An impressive and important work." —JIM MURPHY, TWO-TIME NEWBERY HONOR- AND ROBERT F. SIBERT AWARD-WINNING AUTHOR OF *AN AMERICAN PLAGUE*

"A terrific book." —GEORGE O'CONNOR, *NEW YORK TIMES* BESTSELLING AUTHOR OF THE OLYMPIANS GRAPHIC NOVEL SERIES

★ "A dynamic read deserving of a wide audience."
—*KIRKUS REVIEWS*, STARRED REVIEW

★ "Enlightening." —*BOOKLIST*, STARRED REVIEW

★ "*Crash* will deliver on all levels." —*VOYA*, STARRED REVIEW

UNEQUAL: A Story of America

"Michael Eric Dyson is one of the greatest intellectuals and thought provokers of our time. In this book he and Marc Favreau realize we are the fruit of generations of giants who labored for and demanded a more equal America. Read *Unequal* to learn their stories—and our own."
—COMMON, GRAMMY AWARD-WINNING ARTIST, AUTHOR, ACTOR, AND ACTIVIST

"With clarity and insight, *Unequal* illuminates how racial inequality is built into every aspect of American society."
—ROBIN DiANGELO, #1 BESTSELLING AUTHOR

★ "Empowering, profound, and necessary."
—*SLJ*, STARRED REVIEW

★ "Crucial...A must-read and a must-teach."
—*PUBLISHERS WEEKLY*, STARRED REVIEW

★ "Grounded in evidence and optimistic: uplifts the social power of studying Black American freedom fighters."
—*KIRKUS REVIEWS*, STARRED REVIEW

★ "This is a necessary resource and will inspire students to promote social justice."
—*SLC*, STARRED REVIEW

ATTACKED!

ALSO BY MARC FAVREAU

CRASH
The Great Depression and the
Fall and Rise of America

SPIES
The Secret Showdown
Between America and Russia

UNEQUAL
A Story of America
(with Michael Eric Dyson)

ATTACKED!

Pearl Harbor and the Day War Came to America

MARC FAVREAU

LITTLE, BROWN AND COMPANY
New York   Boston

Little, Brown and Company
Hachette Book Group
1290 Avenue of the Americas, New York, NY 10104
Visit us at LBYR.com

First Edition: November 2023

Little, Brown and Company is a division of Hachette Book Group,
Inc. The Little, Brown name and logo are trademarks of Hachette
Book Group, Inc.

The publisher is not responsible for websites (or their content) that
are not owned by the publisher.

Little, Brown and Company books may be purchased in bulk for
business, educational, or promotional use. For information, please
contact your local bookseller or the Hachette Book Group Special
Markets Department at special.markets@hbgusa.com.

Library of Congress Cataloging-in-Publication Data
Names: Favreau, Marc, 1968– author.
Title: Attacked! : Pearl Harbor and the day war came to
America / Marc Favreau.
Other titles: Pearl Harbor and the day war came to America
Description: First edition. | New York : Little, Brown and
Company, 2023. | Includes bibliographical references and
index. | Audience: Ages 10 and up | Summary: "The attack on
Pearl Harbor unfolds through the actions and perspectives of
American, Japanese, and Hawaiian leaders, soldiers, sailors,
nurses, and civilians." —Provided by publisher.
Identifiers: LCCN 2022060929 | ISBN 9780316592079
(hardcover) | ISBN 9780316592086 (ebook)
Subjects: LCSH: Pearl Harbor (Hawaii), Attack on, 1941—Juvenile
literature. | World War, 1939–1945—Causes—Juvenile literature.
Classification: LCC D767.92 .F38 2023 |
DDC 940.54/26693—dc23/eng/20230111
LC record available at https://lccn.loc.gov/2022060929

ISBNs: 978-0-316-59207-9 (hardcover), 978-0-316-59208-6 (ebook)

Printed in the United States of America

LSC-C

Printing 1, 2023

———◇———

To all my grandparents,
who lived through this story;
I am grateful for what I have
inherited from them.

CONTENTS

PART 3

KEY FIGURES

THE JAPANESE

MITSUO FUCHIDA
A Japanese pilot and flight commander

MINORU GENDA
A Japanese pilot and flight commander

JINICHI GOTO
A Japanese pilot

EMPEROR HIROHITO
The 124th emperor of Japan, who ruled from 1926 until
his death, in 1989

JUZO MORI
A Japanese pilot

ADMIRAL CHUICHI NAGUMO
An admiral in the Imperial Japanese Navy

KAZUO SAKAMAKI
An eighteen-year-old captain of a mini-sub sent to attack
Pearl Harbor

ADMIRAL ISOROKU YAMAMOTO
The highest-ranking officer in the Imperial Japanese Navy

TAKEO YOSHIKAWA
A Japanese spy sent to gather information on America's
military strength in Pearl Harbor

THE AMERICANS

STEPHEN BOWER YOUNG
A sailor aboard the battleship USS *Oklahoma*

MONICA CONTER
A US Army nurse

LIEUTENANT COLONEL JAMES H. DOOLITTLE
An Army Air Forces officer

ALFREDO FERNANDEZ
A Filipino American boy who lived in Damon Tract, a neighborhood near Pearl Harbor

DONALD KELI'INOI
A Hawaiian boy whose family farm was close to Pearl Harbor

PRIVATES JOSEPH LOCKARD AND GEORGE ELLIOTT
US Army radar operators stationed at the remote radar installation at Opana

MARTIN MATTHEWS
A fifteen-year-old US sailor who was visiting a friend on the USS *Arizona* on the morning of December 7

DORIS "DORRIE" MILLER
A mess attendant aboard the battleship USS *West Virginia*

MARY ANN RAMSEY
The daughter of Navy officer Logan Ramsey

ERNEST REID
An Army Air Forces pilot of a B-17 bomber

FRANKLIN DELANO ROOSEVELT
The president of the United States from 1933 until his death in 1945

CHARLES SEHE
A sailor aboard the battleship USS *Nevada*

JOSEPH TAUSSIG JR.
A naval officer aboard the USS *Nevada*

KIMIKO WATANABE
A Japanese American woman living in Honolulu with her son, Dickie, and husband, Kiho, a fisherman

ARTHUR UCHIDA
A Japanese American boy from Honolulu

PROLOGUE
The Ghosts of History

PEARL HARBOR.

The first time I saw these two words, they were at the top of a dreaded pop quiz.

Our fifth-grade math teacher had scrawled them there, and we knew it meant something important—but what? She was growing impatient with how little attention we were paying to her latest lesson. The moment had come, she said, to see what we were made of.

We had no idea what "Pearl Harbor" meant. But for people of my math teacher's generation, I later learned, those two words needed no explaining. They were about the power of surprise, about treachery, and about how something could literally come out of the sky and change your world forever.

Their meaning had a flip side, too: that you must always be prepared.

I later learned that Pearl Harbor was where one of the most important events in all of American history had taken place. But I came to understand it was something more than that: Pearl Harbor was a history lesson, one that neither my teacher nor the America she was born into had ever recovered from. The world was a dangerous place, it said, filled with evil and uncertainty—and America always had to be ready for what came its way.

We had been given no warning that such a math quiz was coming. Were we prepared?

———◇———

On December 7, 1941, four decades before I was handed that math quiz, the Imperial Japanese Navy launched a devastating attack against the US Pacific Fleet, headquartered in Pearl Harbor, Oahu, one of the volcanic islands that make up Hawaii, at the time a US territory.

The United States of America was caught completely off guard. No one could remember anything like this happening before, and Americans vowed never to let it happen again. On street corners, at bus stops, in train stations and school hallways, the same message appeared: REMEMBER PEARL HARBOR.

Pearl Harbor jolted Americans awake. For years, Adolf Hitler's Nazi armies had been on the march across Europe. In 1940, Imperial Japan joined Hitler's "Axis" of dictatorships and was sweeping across Asia. Before Pearl Harbor, most Americans believed that they were safe—insulated from Europe and Asia by two oceans—and could choose when, where, or whether to join the fight for democracy.

After Pearl Harbor, Americans finally got the message about the mortal threat to their country. The United States went to war against the Axis and emerged victorious four years later.

By 1945, America seemed to have avenged Pearl Harbor, once and for all—at great human cost. And Americans everywhere agreed that the United States would never again suffer a deadly surprise attack.

———◇———

As it turned out, however, there would be more Pearl Harbors.

On September 11, 2001, many years after I

took—and promptly failed—my fifth-grade math quiz, another brazen attack came out of the blue and stole the lives of thousands of Americans. This time, it was close to home. I watched from a pier on the west side of Manhattan as the Twin Towers collapsed, killing nearly three thousand people. The acrid smell from the wreckage filled my nose for weeks afterward.

The newspaper headlines the next morning made no mistake of it, calling the terrorist attacks of September 11 a "second Pearl Harbor."

Almost twenty years after that, when I first decided to write this book, the United States had come under assault from a different kind of foe, an invisible and lethal virus that seemed to strike without warning. During that terrible spring of 2020, the surgeon general of the United States announced, "This is going to be our Pearl Harbor moment."

All of these Pearl Harbors had something in common. Despite what seemed (in retrospect) like obvious warning signs, America found itself unprepared, and there was finger-pointing at those people inside the country who, it was believed, allowed this to occur. And in each case, racism—toward the Japanese after Pearl Harbor, toward Muslims after 9/11, or toward China and Asian Americans when the COVID-19 pandemic struck—infected how some Americans decided to assign blame for what had happened.

Why, I asked myself, had the story of Pearl Harbor so powerfully shaped how we understand our present? Why is this history so *unsettled*?

Winston Churchill, the British politician who guided Great Britain through the worst days of World War II as prime minister, remarked that "Those that fail to learn from history are doomed to repeat it."

How should we react when our world changes suddenly? Do we give up or do we dig in and fight back? Do we look for scapegoats, someone to blame, or do we try to help one another?

The real story of Pearl Harbor, it turns out, is more complicated—and much more interesting, tragic, and heroic—than the simplified version handed down to us by our parents and grandparents.

I wrote *Attacked!* to try to get past the headlines, the official memories, and the REMEMBER PEARL HARBOR posters, to tell a story from the words, memories, and experiences of a diverse cast of characters, ordinary people who could never have prepared for a morning when history came crashing out of a blue sky.

PART 1

CHAPTER 1

ONLY A FEW WEEKS INTO THE MOST IMPORTANT MISsion of his life, Takeo Yoshikawa—code name: "Morimura"—had run out of ideas. It was the fall of 1941, and the twenty-eight-year-old Japanese spy was supposed to be gathering as much information as possible about the sprawling American naval base at Pearl Harbor, an enormous, closely guarded military installation on the Hawaiian island of Oahu.

Posing as a Japanese diplomat, Yoshikawa expected to move freely through the city of Honolulu and its surrounding towns. But all of Oahu felt like an armed camp, with military police manning every street corner. As he jostled against strangers on crowded sidewalks, he felt watched. Unfamiliar sounds and voices trailed out of streetcars, bars, pool halls, and shops of every type, and hundreds of American sailors in crisp white uniforms spilled onto the streets at all hours. Yoshikawa scurried past them, avoiding eye contact.

Every night, in the secret code room of the Japanese consulate where Yoshikawa worked undercover, the telegraph machine spewed questions and demands for information.

"How many naval vessels are docked?"

"Where are the battleships and aircraft carriers anchored?"

"How many aircraft are stationed at Ford Island?"

If he didn't deliver answers, it would mean shame for Yoshikawa and for his proud parents.

Yoshikawa had grown up in a family that prized military training. In high school, he was a champion swordsman of kendo, the stick-fighting sport that had helped train samurai warriors for centuries. He followed the tenets of Zen Buddhism and believed that its teachings of self-discipline prepared him well for the fight against Japan's enemies.

He had entered the Imperial Japanese Naval Academy just two years before Japan's fateful decision to become a true empire.

———◆———

Imperial Japan—*Dai Nippon Teikoku*. The island nation of 100 million people had changed faster than any other country in history. Once the territory of medieval samurai lords known as shogun, Japan had morphed into an industrial powerhouse in mere decades.

At a time when European and American empires had carved up Africa and much of Asia, Japan was determined to compete with the great world powers.

In 1931, the Japanese army crossed the Sea of Japan and invaded resource-rich Manchuria, renaming it Manchukuo. Six years later, in 1937, Japan staged an all-out, brutal invasion of China. Blessed by the emperor himself, the war in China became known as "the sacred war," or *seisen*. Many Japanese citizens believed firmly that their country's military conquests were a righteous quest for glory.

On December 13, 1937, Japanese troops captured the Chinese city of Nanjing and slaughtered as many as 300,000 soldiers and civilians. Western news reports of the atrocities shocked many Americans, turning public opinion in the United States sharply against Japan's new push into Asia.

Japan pressed on with its war aims. Under the rallying cry of "Asia for Asians," Japan announced what it called the Greater East Asia Co-Prosperity Sphere (under Japanese leadership). Japanese propaganda criticized Western powers for their own imperialism in Asia—and the United States for its racist treatment of its citizens of color, particularly those of Asian descent. But in reality, these messages covered up Japan's ruthless treatment of the Asian peoples newly under its control.

Japan soon joined with Nazi Germany and Fascist Italy, forming a military pact in September 1940. Each country in the Axis pledged to go to war to protect the others.

As Japan's military chiefs dreamed of an empire spanning the Pacific, they saw only one real obstacle: a single US naval base in a shallow harbor, bristling with battleships, aircraft carriers, and thousands of American sailors. No other military force in the Pacific had the strength—or was close enough—to block Japan's ambitions.

Japan's military leaders decided they needed to know more about what its main enemy across the Pacific was up to. They sent an unassuming, slightly nervous young spy to find out.

The spy Takeo Yoshikawa in an undated photo.

On Yoshikawa's first attempt to get a closer look at the big naval base at Pearl Harbor, his taxi driver sped up as they passed the wrought-iron perimeter fence. He explained to Yoshikawa that the Navy was on the lookout for spies, and that police officers lurked in the bushes to arrest anyone—even an innocent cabdriver—trying to peer inside.

The Navy wasn't taking chances: on nearby Hickam Field air base, where hundreds of America's best fighter aircraft were parked close together out in the open, armed guards stood by to protect them from potential sneak attacks by Japanese secret agents. The Navy's commanders reasoned that they would be safest this way.

If the Americans found out who Yoshikawa really was, it would be life in prison—or death by firing squad.

———◇———

After a particularly stressful day, Yoshikawa made his way up to the Shunchoro Teahouse in Alewa Heights in Honolulu, to relax over whiskies and soda.

It was a beautiful evening, and the Shunchoro's main room had a large picture window looking out toward the ocean. Laid out before Yoshikawa was an unobstructed view of the US Navy base at Pearl Harbor. "Lights were flickering all over," he later remarked, "making it look like an enormous starfish."

That very evening, a new plan took shape in Yoshikawa's mind.

Although Hawaii was an American territory, much of it was culturally Japanese. While tourist brochures touted Hawaii as a vacation paradise for white visitors, two-thirds of the island's 260,000 full-time residents were descended from Japanese parents or grandparents—men and women who had immigrated to pick pineapples or cut sugarcane on large plantations where thousands of poorly paid workers toiled in the hot sun.

With the right disguise, Yoshikawa realized, he could blend in.

Donning a Hawaiian shirt and cap, the spy began to make daily forays onto the streets of Honolulu, listening for bits and pieces of information about the US fleet.

He went swimming, making note of coral reefs that might prevent a boat from reaching the shore safely.

He read the local papers, carefully clipping information about admirals, captains...and their ships.

Abandoning his diplomatic cover, he sometimes worked as a dishwasher at the Pearl Harbor officers' club, pricking up his ears for gossip.

He played the tourist, taking glass-bottom boat tours, going on hikes, and even purchasing tickets for charter flights that offered a view of all of Oahu from several thousand feet up.

He took measurements of the harbor depth, breathing through a reed to stay underwater for long periods of time without attracting attention.

And he returned again and again to the Shunchoro Teahouse. He even took to renting a room with a clear view of the harbor, which he would scan carefully through a set of binoculars. Under the spy's watchful gaze, planes took off and landed, and ships of all sizes came and went.

All of this information he committed to memory, never carrying a camera, pen, or notepad. At night, in the cramped telegraph room in the consulate, he would carefully encode his daily catch of information and wire it to Tokyo.

Over weeks and months, Yoshikawa assembled a detailed picture of every military installation on Oahu—including all the ships stationed in Pearl Harbor. He could even predict their movements with accuracy.

But he could not answer one simple question: Why did his bosses in Tokyo need all this information?

CHAPTER 2

ON SATURDAY, DECEMBER 6, 1941, AN EXHAUSTED
President Franklin Delano Roosevelt retired to his study
after hosting thirty-two dinner guests in the White
House dining room.

Months of negotiations were taking their toll on the
president. He had used a wheelchair since contracting
polio, and throughout 1941 FDR had sunk into bouts of
anemia, the flu, and other illnesses.

Over the past eighteen months, the world FDR
thought he knew had crumbled.

In May and June of 1940, Adolf Hitler's Nazi armies
rolled into the Netherlands, Belgium, Luxembourg, and
France (having already invaded Poland, Czechoslova-
kia, and Austria). Now eyeing Britain, Hitler launched

his fearsome air force, the Luftwaffe, in an all-out assault on England.

The British Royal Air Force managed to halt the Luftwaffe's advance, but German bombers still pounded British cities. Would all of Europe fall to the Nazi menace? And would Hitler then set his sights on the United States? To FDR, there seemed to be little he could do about it.

A powerful group of "isolationists," people who believed that the United States should not get tangled up in international affairs, conspired to block FDR's moves to support England's war against Hitler. The America First Committee handed out leaflets, bumper stickers, and pins by the hundreds of thousands, and flooded the White House mailroom with postcards and letters opposing any intervention in a "European war."

In the summer of 1941, the forces of Imperial Japan made a bold move in the Pacific. In July, Japanese troops seized a group of airfields in southern Indochina (now Vietnam and Cambodia), an action that put them in position to attack farther south, toward the British colony of Singapore, the oil-rich Dutch East Indies (now Indonesia), and even Australia.

In an attempt to interrupt Japan's plans, Roosevelt

froze all of Japan's financial assets in the United States and placed a total embargo on the sale of oil to the island nation. This would make it impossible for Japan—a nation that imported *more than 80 percent* of the petroleum it needed—to run its economy and far-flung military.

Japanese leaders estimated that they could last eighteen months without American oil. Either America had to give in or Japan had to push south to secure its own source of petroleum. It was a classic standoff, and the clock was ticking.

For the remainder of that summer and through the fall, talks between Japan and the United States dragged on, with neither side giving an inch.

As far as FDR was concerned, slow-moving negotiations were exactly what America needed. War in the Pacific would come eventually, he believed—but where? With the isolationists blocking his attempts to increase military spending, the president knew that America was in no shape to hold back Hitler, let alone Imperial Japan.

FDR needed time. Time to build up his armed forces. Time to persuade his stubborn fellow citizens to take the Axis threat seriously. Time to keep Japan from making rash moves into Thailand, Singapore, or

Indonesia—or, worse, into the American-held Philippines, where the small American force deployed there would be no match for Japan's powerful army.

The flames of war licked at America's doorstep. To the east, FDR tried to douse them by sending weapons and supplies to America's main ally, Great Britain. To the west, with little time to spare, he did the one thing that might give Japan second thoughts about igniting a war in the Pacific: In the fall of 1941, the president ordered battleships, aircraft carriers, fighter aircraft, and Army personnel to reinforce a lonely US Navy base on the small Hawaiian island of Oahu named Pearl Harbor.

Thousands of miles from Japan, Pearl Harbor was not at risk of being attacked itself, FDR believed—and his advisers agreed. But by sending American ships and planes to Oahu, America was sending a powerful message to Japan.

The United States was ready.

———◆———

If he walked a short way down his farm's dirt road, nine-year-old Donald Keli'inoi could just make out the dark shapes of battleships. They came and went from Pearl Harbor, belching black clouds from their smokestacks.

An aerial view of the US naval
base at Pearl Harbor.

The constant whine of plane engines as they took off, landed, and performed aerial maneuvers overhead played like a soundtrack to his quiet, lonely life.

The Keli'inoi family's ten-acre farm sat only three miles from the big Navy base, but it may as well have been on a different planet. When a car came up the road, the family would rush outside, hoping for visitors to break the monotony of their lives.

"Day in, day out, you just saw each other. A visitor was a major event," Donald said.

The western shore of Pearl Harbor bordered an area of flat, saltwater farms owned by hardworking Hawaiian families like Donald Keli'inoi's, descendants of the island's original inhabitants. The United States had invaded the island kingdom just over forty years earlier, deposing its leader and annexing Hawaii as its colony. In the years since then, white Americans gobbled up the best lands for themselves, pushing once-thriving Hawaiians to shabby backwaters such as Pu'uloa Farms, where the Keli'inois tilled the ground for a meager living.

Donald's home was about as far away from an island paradise as one could imagine. His family's ten-acre vegetable farm was so remote that they had no mailing address: letters were simply sent to the Keli'inoi Farm in Pu'uloa. The wider world seemed very, very far away.

And yet, just over the horizon from Donald's quiet life, things were getting louder, more hectic, and more ominous.

Three miles to the east, hundreds of new sailors arrived every week at the largest naval base in the world. Battleships, destroyers, aircraft carriers, and smaller Navy vessels of all kinds anchored in the calm waters of Pearl Harbor, and launches ferrying sailors and officers in crisp white uniforms crisscrossed between them at all hours. And on the runways of Ford Island and nearby Hickam Field, long-range bombers, fighter planes, and reconnaissance aircraft kept ground crews scrambling from daybreak to nightfall.

From his nearby perch in Pu'uloa, Donald Keli'inoi could see something was afoot.

Donald could not have known it, but events unfolding halfway around the world were about to turn his life upside down.

———◆———

Across the water from the Keli'inoi farm, another young person was being pulled into Pearl Harbor's orbit, drawn in by currents over which she had no control.

The last place on earth Mary Ann Ramsey wanted to go was smack-dab in the middle of a Navy base. She had just graduated from high school in Philadelphia in June 1941 and, after a lifetime of moving around as the child of a naval officer, she finally had friends and a place to call home. It had been the first time she lived in one place for more than a year. What did she care about Hawaiian beaches, and what did she know about a war brewing on the other side of the globe?

But once again, she let adults uproot her life.

Ramsey's dad was chief of staff to Vice Admiral Patrick Bellinger, the man newly in charge of the naval air station on Ford Island, which sat in the middle of Pearl Harbor. Logan Ramsey had already flown to Oahu earlier that month, ahead of his family—one of thousands of officers and enlisted men and women shipped off to Pearl Harbor as part of FDR's strategy to keep Japan's ambitions in check.

And so Mary Ann and her mother made the long trek alone, a week by train to San Francisco, and then five grueling days by steamship to Honolulu. Mary's attitude did not make the trip any easier. "I remained unreconciled to my Hawaiian prospects on all counts," she said, "and was adolescent glum most of the trip west."

When the boat approached the dock in Oahu, however, Mary Ann's mood lifted for the first time in weeks. Ships arriving in Hawaii from the mainland were treated to a special welcome of confetti and streamers. As Mary and her mother descended the gangplank, her father rushed toward them with traditional Hawaiian flower necklaces called leis.

And then there were the sailors, thousands of them, in white uniforms and trademark caps, bantering in every possible American accent. "We were literally surrounded by them," she recalled, "their ships berthed about us in a seemingly invincible necklace of gray steel." Pearl Harbor was almost like its own country, bustling and busy, noisy and alive, all of it protected by the most powerful military on earth.

Mary Ann's family settled into a comfortable, tropical-style house set near those of Admiral Bellinger and his staff, on the eastern corner of Ford Island. She could stand on her porch and gaze out over Battleship Row, as it was nicknamed. It was so close that in the evenings, she sat and listened to the soundtracks of movies being shown on the deck of the USS *Arizona*.

Maybe, she thought, life in Hawaii wouldn't be so bad after all. Maybe she could finally stay in one place for good.

CHAPTER 3

ON NOVEMBER 17, 1941, KAZUO SAKAMAKI learned that he would be leaving Japan for the first time in his life, on a secret mission. He was departing the very next day—his eighteenth birthday.

For most of that year, rumors had spread like wildfire about where Japan might go to war next. That afternoon, Kazuo's commanding officer put any doubts to rest.

"War with America!" the officer exclaimed.

Japan's leaders, Kazuo learned, had decided to launch a mission to demolish the US Pacific Fleet. A surprise attack, they believed, was their only chance to succeed against the might of the US Navy. With the right strategy, smaller could defeat larger.

Kazuo Sakamaki had entered Japan's elite Naval Academy when he was only fourteen years old, having dreamed of military service ever since he watched soldiers from his village march off to fight Japan's wars of conquest in China. Like most boys of his generation, he believed profoundly that Japan was not only a superior nation but also a force for good in the world. He was willing to fight for those beliefs—and for his emperor.

On graduation, Kazuo joined a small group of specially trained captains. Over months of intensive instruction, he became an expert in handling Japan's surprise weapon, a miniature, two-man submarine armed with torpedoes that could sink a battleship or aircraft carrier at short range.

The mini-sub was small enough to slip undetected into a heavily guarded harbor, able to deliver a lethal blow with no warning. Kazuo imagined the powerful American ships sinking in their own harbor, defeated by Japan's superior know-how and by brave warriors like himself.

The Japanese Navy built five mini-subs, each one operated by a two-person crew. Because the mini-subs were too small to cross the Pacific Ocean, each one would be mounted on a much larger submarine—a mother ship that would carry the mini-sub and its crew to its final destination.

As they prepared to leave, Kazuo and his fellow

sailors were called to a meeting with Admiral Mitsumi Shimizu, the commander of their entire fleet.

"One mistake on the part of any one of you may be fatal to all of us," the admiral lectured them. "The Sixth Fleet, the navy itself, and the whole country. I trust in your loyalty and ability."

Kazuo left the meeting feeling dazed. He realized, at that moment, how much responsibility rested on his shoulders. And he understood, in his bones, that he might never return to Japan alive.

That evening, Kazuo took a walk with a classmate through the port city of Kure, near the naval base where he was stationed. They passed a store window displaying bottles of perfume.

"Here is something we must have," Kazuo said to his friend. It seemed like a strange suggestion at first, but Kazuo explained that throughout history, Japanese warriors dressed in their finest armor and perfumed themselves before going to war.

The next morning, before his departure, Kazuo wrote what he thought might be his final letter to his parents.

I am now leaving. I owe you, my parents, a debt I shall never be able to repay. Whatever

may happen to me, it is in the service of our
country that I go.

"I was saying good-bye to all things to which a normal person clings," Kazuo recalled. "I had made up my mind to cease being normal. I, Kazuo Sakamaki, was being buried as of that moment. A skipper of a secret submarine going out in the service of his country was dictating that letter."

He swallowed his tears.

At noon, Kazuo steered his mini-sub out of the harbor. Once at sea, it was attached to the decks of the larger submarine that would carry it across the ocean. That same day, he began the long journey east, across the Pacific, to Pearl Harbor.

———◆———

While men like Kazuo Sakamaki understood the small part they would play in Japan's dramatic attack on America, there was no way any of them could know the immense scope of the government's plans. Japan's military planners dubbed it Operation Z. In the fall of 1941, on the southern island of Kyushu, far away from the prying eyes of Western agents, some of the best pilots in the world conducted mock attack runs over a bay not unlike Pearl Harbor. Kazuo Sakamaki and his fellow crew would strike at the enemy's soft underbelly; Japan's finest airmen would mount an attack head-on.

They trained at all hours, seven days a week, no matter the weather. It was to be a mission, the men were told, like no other in the history of Japan.

Their commanding officer was Minoru Genda, a daring upstart young commander who believed passionately that air power held the key to Japan's imperial ambitions. Genda put Lieutenant Mitsuo Fuchida in command of the First Air Fleet and charged him with training the squadron that would lead any attack against America.

Together, Fuchida and Genda hatched a plan that most military leaders—on both sides of the Pacific—assumed would never work. It all depended on a weapon they dubbed *gyorai*, or "thunderfish": large, oblong torpedoes mounted beneath single-engine planes each manned by three aviators.

There was just one problem with that plan.

Aside from the vast distances that separated it from any enemy, Pearl Harbor had one natural defense. The entire harbor was barely forty feet deep, a fact confirmed by the spy Yoshikawa's swimming expeditions that fall.

Normally, a torpedo dive-bomber would release its lethal weapon at a safe distance, from a safe altitude, and then veer away. Once the torpedo dived beneath the surface, its spinning propeller and stabilizers would put it on a straight path toward the intended target.

But Japan's military experts worried that in water as shallow as Pearl Harbor's, the torpedoes would immediately get stuck in the sandy ocean bottom.

For this very same reason, American military leaders believed that ships moored in Pearl Harbor were immune from an airborne torpedo attack. They were so sure of this that the American fleet wasn't protected by torpedo nets—underwater fences that caused torpedoes to detonate on impact, before they could damage a ship.

From their base on Kyushu, Genda and Fuchida's crews came up with a makeshift solution that turned out to be deadly effective. They attached small wooden fins to each torpedo, something that prevented the two-ton weapons from dropping too quickly when they hit the water. They would churn the waters just below the surface. It was a terrifying sight for whoever might be at the receiving end, as the white wake bore down on its target like a shark hunting its prey.

But in order for this to work, Fuchida's pilots had to drop the *gyorai* from an impossibly low altitude, while almost skimming the surface of choppy seas. Yet if the propellers of their aircraft were to hit the water, the pilot and crew risked crashing nose-first, which would lead to a near-certain watery death.

Finally, in late November of 1941, the training sessions came to an end and the crews were assigned to bunks in a fleet of aircraft carriers moored in the bay.

On the evening of November 23, a voice blared over the loudspeakers in each ship, ordering the aircrews to report for an important announcement. The wait was over, at last.

"On December 8," their commanding officer informed them, "we will attack and destroy the US fleet at Pearl Harbor." (Because of the international date line, December 8 in Japan would be December 7 in Hawaii.)

Their moment had come. Everything—years of training and sacrifice, months spent away from their families—now made sense. Operation Z was the tip of the spear that would knock down the Americans once and for all.

They departed three days later. Every one of the aircraft carriers in the Japanese Navy joined the strike force: the *Akagi*, *Soryu*, *Kaga*, *Hiryu*, *Shokaku*, and *Zuikaku*. Together, they hauled more than four hundred fighter aircraft and crews, along with thousands of sailors and support personnel. A protective cordon of defensive and supply ships would guide this precious cargo across the North Pacific, following a route through choppy, wintry seas.

Japan was launching its most powerful weapons against America, risking the survival of its entire fleet for a single knockout blow. It was a bold, almost reckless plan. Japan's leaders believed that if they could destroy the US Pacific Fleet, America would lose the will and the means to fight. With the United States on the sidelines, the imperial forces would sweep south into Malaya, Singapore, and Indonesia, capturing vital oil fields and clinching Japan's dominance over all of East Asia.

Japan had gambled its dreams of empire on this one secret operation.

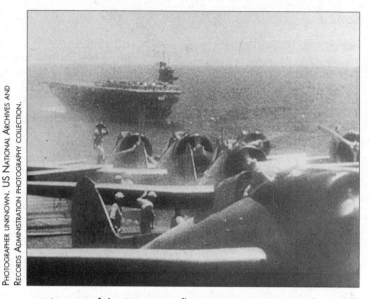

A view of the Japanese fleet as it steams toward
Pearl Harbor; the aircraft carrier *Soryu*
can be seen in the rear.

———◆———

In the long days at sea, hours went by slowly as the steel
ships pitched and rolled on dark waves.

"She was also making strange groaning noises, as
if fighting for her life against a sea that would tear
her apart," the pilot Juzo Mori said of his ship. "One
moment her bow would be completely submerged in a
giant wave, the next her enormous bulk would rear up

out of the water like it was nothing at all. It was an awesome sight that never ceased to amaze me."

Three dozen vessels cruised silently, a massive flotilla spread out over miles of icy waters. To avoid being discovered by a fishing boat—or, worse, by an enemy ship—Japanese navigators followed a route far from land or shipping lanes.

Success depended on total secrecy—and complete surprise.

Foul weather and dense cloud cover helped them, but the sailors and airmen belowdecks suffered from the constant rising and falling. Some nights, the sea was so rough that the crew had to be served balls of rice, because it would be too hard to handle dinner with chopsticks.

There would be no refueling stops on this secret journey. Instead, the fleet's fuel tanker ships had to maneuver alongside the larger fighting vessels to pump diesel into their tanks through long, flexible hoses. More than once, sailors slipped on oil-slick decks and fell to their deaths into the ocean. The convoy traveled on a strict schedule, in total radio silence: There was no calling for help, and no turning back.

During the long crossing from Japan to the waters near Oahu on the *Akagi*, Mori and his fellow pilots studied a diorama of Pearl Harbor, which included scale models of each of the US Navy ships moored there and their precise location. Painstakingly assembled using intelligence from the spy Morimura's observations, the model helped the pilots focus on the dangerous mission that lay before them.

Pilots passed the time by going down to the plane hangar and slipping into their aircraft cockpits. They would close their eyes and try to imagine how the attack would unfold, moment by moment. They had trained for every possibility. And yet they knew that anything could go wrong.

Approaching the end of their journey, the men calmed themselves by recalling the purpose of their historic mission. "We would be the foundation stone for the eternal glory of our nation," pilot Juzo Mori reflected.

On Thursday, December 4, the fleet reached a point several hundred miles to the north of Hawaii, and carved a wide turn south, heading into warmer waters, and toward victory...or disaster.

CHAPTER 4

Stephen Bower Young spent December 6 basking in the sunshine reflecting off Pearl Harbor. A sailor aboard the battleship USS *Oklahoma*, Young had spent much of his life shivering through frigid December temperatures in New England. He had only recently arrived in the South Pacific, and the tropical winter climate suited him just fine.

The *Oklahoma* nestled alongside the USS *Maryland* and nudged just behind the *West Virginia*. Five more battleships were moored near them: the *Arizona*, *Pennsylvania*, *Tennessee*, *California*, and *Nevada*. Battleship Row housed most of the United States Navy's firepower in the Pacific Ocean.

Nearly six hundred feet long and almost one hundred feet wide at the middle, the hulking battleship

Oklahoma resembled a floating, armored island. Fourteen hundred sailors lived and worked below the *Oklahoma*'s armored decks.

Below the waterline, the ship's massive hull wore a specially designed belt of steel. At a foot thick, this protective band shielded the battleship's vital organs—boilers, gunpowder, and cannon shells—from an enemy's torpedoes.

Ten huge cannons mounted on four turrets extended across the *Oklahoma*'s decks. Each turret was so large that it required sixty men to operate.

The ship's engineers had designed the *Oklahoma* as an impenetrable fortress, and nobody had any reason to doubt them.

"No one could sink a battleship," one sailor remarked to himself.

———◇———

At the opposite end of Battleship Row, Charles Sehe had kitchen duty, scrubbing pots and pans in the scullery of the USS *Nevada*.

Sehe enlisted in the US Navy on Thanksgiving Day 1940, for the simple reason that the Navy offered him a full meal on the day he signed up.

Charles Sehe in his US Navy uniform.

"I am what you call a Depression-era child," he said, having spent his teen years scrounging for food. He was only seventeen when he joined, so his mother had to sign the enlistment papers for him.

Sehe was one of the 200,000 boys and girls who enlisted in America's armed forces in the 1940s. An altered birth certificate added a few years to a child's age—enough to get past eager recruiters. Like Sehe, these were all children of the Great Depression, most of whom were accustomed to the grinding poverty that came with America's worst economic collapse.

Even with war clouds gathering over Europe, finding a warm berth on a Navy warship—with three square meals a day—seemed like a dream.

———◇———

Above deck on the *Nevada*, Joe Taussig stood watch. He was twenty-one, freshly graduated from the United States Naval Academy in Annapolis, Maryland. But that made him one of the older crew members on the sprawling ship. With most of the senior officers ashore for a day of shopping and tourism, the average age of the *Nevada* crew on board was only nineteen. It was, literally, a battleship manned mostly by teenagers.

For such a young man, Taussig had known the Navy for a very long time. His father, Joseph Taussig Sr., was an admiral and a graduate of the Naval Academy, too, as was Joe's grandfather. Taussigs had been in the Navy without interruption since before the Civil War.

Joe had grown up around ships. His father commanded a battleship group, and during the summers, Joe traveled with him, as was the custom among the sons of senior officers. In the middle of the Great Depression, the Taussigs lived a life of uncommon privilege, with cooks, maids, and elegant living quarters.

By the time he was ten years old, Joe had the run of some of the United States' most advanced fighting vessels, where he learned to navigate, tie sailing knots—and play cards and swear—like a true sailor.

"I was getting a real education," Joe said. A career in the Navy was in his bones.

He felt he was on the cusp of something new, something big—something that would make good on his family legacy.

———◆———

Forward and to the left of the *Nevada*, deep in the bowels of the battleship *West Virginia*, Doris ("Dorrie") Miller was learning that the Navy's benefits were not doled out equally.

Miller had known hard work for as long as he could remember. As a child, he washed dishes, fished, hunted squirrels, and even took a mail-order course in taxidermy. But in the lean years of the late 1930s, in dirt-poor Waco, Texas, a seventeen-year-old African

American boy could barely earn enough to feed himself. So just after his eighteenth birthday, Dorrie traveled to Dallas and signed up for a six-year tour in the US Navy.

Dorrie left the South and sailed the world, but he didn't leave Jim Crow behind: The US Navy rigidly segregated sailors by race, with Black men like Dorrie stuck in the lowest, most menial jobs. When the *West Virginia* visited ports of call in New Zealand and Australia, Dorrie had to stay aboard ship, owing to the whites-only policies of both countries.

As a mess attendant second class, Dorrie waited on officers in the mess hall, pulled laundry duty, and even shined shoes when ordered to. Black men throughout the US military were denied fighting roles despite their willingness to enlist in large numbers. An African American newspaper in Waco quipped that "the only way Negroes can die in Uncle Sam's democratic Navy is slinging hash."

Still, Dorrie did his best to get ahead. Even if the Navy didn't allow him to fight for his country, "it beats sitting around Waco working as a busboy, going nowhere," he said. Maybe he'd see the world, make a name for himself— and at the very least, send some money home.

———◇———

As with Dorrie Miller, military service offered Monica Conter a way to get out of a small town. Conter left behind Apalachicola, Florida, and joined the Army Nurse Corps—one of the few options open to women hoping to serve in the US military. Her first assignment took her to Walter Reed Hospital in Washington, DC, where she was quickly spotted by a recruiter for Army nurses.

Conter's photograph appeared on recruitment posters all over the United States that year. In 1941, the entire US Army had just under one thousand active-duty nurses. With war engulfing the globe, some of the nation's military leaders feared that they would need many more in the years to come.

"It was very exciting," Conter remembered, "[but] I was dying to get overseas, and I kept bugging them about when I was going to get to Hawaii."

In July, Conter got her answer. The Army assigned her to Hickam Hospital, a brand-new building that had been constructed as part of FDR's buildup of American forces in Pearl Harbor. It had thirty beds, the latest equipment, and a covered porch that faced the water.

Hospital duty was light in Pearl Harbor, with an occasional sprained ankle or case of pneumonia, leaving Conter and her fellow nurses plenty of free evenings to explore.

Throughout the fall of 1941, as more and more sailors, nurses, marines, pilots, and other military personnel arrived in Oahu, news of the simmering conflict with the Axis powers sometimes cast shadows over the thrill of being posted in the South Pacific.

A week earlier, Conter had written a letter home to her parents in Apalachicola.

> *This war situation is really something. We have been on alert for a week now and don't [know] when we are coming off. It looks quite "bad" at times. . . .*

But the sun had a way of driving away the clouds in Hawaii. By Saturday, December 6, the alert had been called off—and the warnings lifted. Conter and fellow nurses celebrated by making dates with some Navy officers.

Many people remembered that Saturday evening as warm and clear, fading into a perfect tropical winter night. "There were Navy people all over the place,"

Conter recalled. "The fleets were in. So with that we decided to walk, and we went down to the harbor: It was the most beautiful sight I've ever seen. All the battleships and the lights with the reflection on the water.

"We were just overwhelmed," she said. "I'll just never forget it."

———◇———

Hours later, about ten miles off the coast of Oahu, the submarine carrying Kazuo Sakamaki's mini-sub rose to the surface. Kazuo could see the lights of Honolulu, glimmering in the distance. Someone turned on a radio. American voices and jazz music echoed through the ship—a sudden reminder, if anyone had forgotten, of the mission that lay ahead of them that night.

The time had come, finally, for everything he had trained for. Kazuo and his assistant checked their supplies on the mini-sub and made final preparations for separating from the mother ship. They climbed into their small cockpit, sealed the hatch, and were released into the dark waters.

"My family, my village, the navy, and my country— they were depending on me," Kazuo thought. "From this moment I was on my own. The target was right ahead. I had to make good. If I should succeed, well and good. If I should fail? No! I could not fail."

"On to Pearl Harbor!" he shouted as the little sub plunged into the water, steering straight for the narrow harbor entrance and the fleet of ships beyond.

CHAPTER 5

THAT SAME EVENING, HIS MIND PULLED IN TOO MANY directions, President Roosevelt tried to distract himself in his private office by poring over his stamp collection.

Earlier in the day, in a final, last-ditch effort to prevent an oil-starved Japan from launching a wider war in the Pacific, he sent a personal telegram to the Japanese emperor Hirohito. "I am confident that both of us," he pleaded, "have a sacred duty to restore traditional amity and prevent further death and destruction." Even knowing that war was likely, FDR hoped for peace.

And then, at nine thirty, an Army messenger arrived at the White House with a sealed pouch, containing a freshly intercepted message from the government in Tokyo to the Japanese embassy in Washington.

American eavesdroppers routinely read top secret

communications from Tokyo to Washington and were able to decipher them thanks to the success of their expert codebreakers. This particular secret message informed Japan's diplomats that the Japanese government had finally rejected American demands to withdraw from China and Southeast Asia. The document ended abruptly, because the eavesdropping team had not yet decoded the final, fourteenth part of the Japanese cable. But Roosevelt understood at that moment that diplomacy between the United States and Japan had finally run its course.

"This means war," he said aloud.

The only question was when—and where?

———◆———

Early the next morning, the remaining piece of the decoded cable from Tokyo to Washington finally arrived.

It was delivered by hand to the White House and to other high-level officials in the US government.

One of these was Colonel Rufus Bratton, chief of the Far Eastern Section of the Military Intelligence Division of the War Department—a man who had been paying close attention to Japan's actions for years.

The secret cable instructed the Japanese ambassador

to meet with the US secretary of state no earlier than one PM, Eastern Standard Time, that very day, and to present Japan's final response to the United States. Then, ominously, it ordered the ambassador, Kichisaburo Nomura, to return to the embassy and destroy its secret code machines.

US officials had been poring over cryptic messages from Japan's leaders for the better part of a year. But to Bratton, this latest message was different.

Confused and alarmed, Bratton immediately sent a breathless message to the personal assistant of General George C. Marshall, the secretary of the Army: "The General needs to see this now." But on Sunday mornings, Marshall liked to take long horseback rides around the capital.

Ninety minutes passed. At last, Marshall charged through the front door of his office and assembled his aides to help make sense of the declassified message.

What could such a deadline mean? Why insist on waiting until one o'clock on a Sunday afternoon to inform the United States that Japan was rejecting all its ten demands? And why would Japan want to destroy its own precious code machines, something that an embassy did only when a country was going to war and was concerned about its technology falling into enemy hands?

They agreed that Japanese forces were already on the move and that the delayed message was intended to enable the Japanese military to launch a surprise attack somewhere in the Pacific. Whether it might be against America or one of its allies, no one knew for sure.

Whatever the precise meaning, Marshall sounded the alarm. Moving quickly, the general scrawled a handwritten message to the top brass in all of America's West Coast and Pacific military bases. "Be on the alert accordingly," he wrote.

One of his aides rushed the message to the Army Signals Center. From there, it was radioed across the United States to the Presidio in San Francisco. It was then relayed to American forces in the Panama Canal Zone, and finally across the ocean to General MacArthur's headquarters in the Philippines.

But because of dense clouds and rough weather over the North Pacific, the wireless transmission to Pearl Harbor could not get through. Precious minutes ticked by. In a pinch, Marshall's staff did the only thing they could think of—they sent a regular Western Union telegram to

Honolulu, to be delivered by hand to Admiral Husband Kimmel, the commander of the US Navy base.

In the meantime, Kimmel remained in the dark.

———◇———

Just north of San Francisco, the engines of eight B-17 bombers, known as "Flying Fortresses," growled as the big planes rolled toward the runway for takeoff, one by one, at fifteen-minute intervals. At this late hour, just past ten thirty PM, only the plane's navigation lights could be seen, blinking in the darkness around Hamilton Field.

When his turn came, Ernest Reid's bomber lumbered into the air. Using the stars as a guide, Reid's navigator set a western course. Another squadron of four B-17s took off from a different airfield and joined Reid's group high over the Pacific Ocean.

Reid had logged just over one hundred hours as his B-17's copilot. The Army Air Forces were scrambling to train and equip hundreds of new pilots and bomber crews, most of them destined for England and the fight against Hitler. Reid drew a different straw. He was on his way to Pearl Harbor.

Reid and his fellow flight crews were part of FDR's plan for dealing with Japan in the fall of 1941. Their thirteen-hour flight to Pearl Harbor was just the first leg of a five-thousand-mile journey to Clark Field in the Philippines, a US air base outside the capital city of Manila. If his generals could get enough B-17s to Clark Field and other air bases in the Philippines, FDR reasoned, then America might well blunt Imperial Japan's ambitions to invade Southeast Asia.

That night, each of the powerful war machines lofted into the sky more or less toothless. Expecting no enemies on the way to Hawaii, the crews had disassembled their guns and packed them in Cosmoline, a special grease to protect their metal parts from rust. And in any case, the planes carried no ammunition; they would pick it up in Hawaii before taking off again for the final leg of the trip to Clark Field.

Across the ocean, a Navy officer in Pearl Harbor telephoned the radio station KGMB in Honolulu to ask the DJ to stay on the air all night so that the B-17 pilots would use the radio signal to home in on Oahu as they approached the islands.

That evening and through the next morning,

ATTACKED!

December 7, the gentle sounds of luau music rippled through the airwaves around Hawaii.

———◇———

Mitsuo Fuchida woke at five AM Hawaii time on Sunday, December 7 (ten AM Washington time). He'd slept only a few hours, but he leaped out of his bunk, eager for the day to begin. He dressed quickly and went above to the pilots' briefing room.

The Japanese fleet had spent twelve hard days at sea, sailing in near-total radio silence. They had arrived, finally, at the staging point for Operation Z—230 miles north of the island of Oahu, a distance that the planes lashed to the decks could cross in a mere ninety minutes.

But the scene above deck did not inspire confidence. The aircraft carrier *Akagi* plunged through rough seas, the ship's bow slamming into the water each time it lifted and dropped on the waves.

The time for the attack on Pearl Harbor had come.

"Japan would now wield the sword of righteousness," pilot Juzo Mori thought to himself.

The *Akagi* briefing room was so crammed with pilots that some had to listen from the hallway. A chalkboard on the wall showed a drawing of the location of the American fleet only twenty-four hours earlier—courtesy of the spy Takeo Yoshikawa.

No navy had ever launched so many planes under such rough conditions, and in reality, Fuchida and his fellow pilots had little sense of what they would find in the skies over Oahu. Were the Americans waiting for them? Would they die on this mission?

No one knew for certain.

After the briefing, men gathered momentarily at small Shinto shrines, saying a final prayer for good fortune—followed in some cases by a bracing shot of sake, a Japanese rice wine.

Some men tightened handmade "thousand-stitch" belts around their waists. Called *senninbari*, these ceremonial white garments had been stitched with red thread by warriors' wives, mothers, sisters, and daughters to give the pilots good luck during battle.

Up on the open carrier deck, crews had readied Fuchida's plane. The entire tail section of his three-man bomber was painted yellow, with three bright red lines visible from a distance—marks of the attack operation's general commander. As Fuchida climbed the ladder to his cockpit, a crew member presented him with a

Japanese crews cheer as a fighter prepares
for takeoff on the aircraft carrier
Akagi on December 7, 1941.

hachimaki, a ceremonial white headband to wear during
the attack. Fuchida tied it around his flight helmet, and
it fluttered in the wind.

"Start your engines."

The command echoed from the flight deck. Each
plane in the first squadron flicked on its flight lamp,
and soon the whole carrier was illuminated by the small,
quivering lights.

The enormous *Akagi* turned its rudder so that the
planes could take off into the heavy wind, giving them

enough lift on the short runway. The five other aircraft carriers, cruising in formation, followed its lead.

To avoid ditching into the churning seas, a plane had to time its takeoff exactly right, accelerating just as the bow of the ship lifted skyward on a wave.

"My back was wet with sweat," pilot Juzo Mori recalled. "When the launch officer raised his flag, I slammed the throttle wide open and we thundered off the deck into the inky black sky. Looking back at the ship, I could just make out the sailors' waving caps and the other planes taking to the air. On the bridge I could see the captain and his officers, their caps waving over their heads. You can depend on us, I said to myself."

Once in the air, the planes flew wide circles around the fleet, gradually forming groups behind their squadron leaders as more and more of their fellow pilots took off from the carrier decks. In less than an hour, the first wave of attackers—353 dive-bombers, torpedo bombers, and horizontal bombers, all of them loaded with weapons and ammunition—fell into formation over the open ocean, with Fuchida leading the way.

The sun was already coming up, and to Mitsuo Fuchida its rays seemed to resemble the flag of Imperial Japan. At six fifteen, Fuchida slid open his canopy and raised his arms in a triumphant gesture. Behind him, the largest air armada in history roared toward the island of Oahu.

———◆———

At 7:33 AM, Hawaiian time, a bicycle messenger at the Western Union office in downtown Honolulu picked up the teletype message warning of a possible Japanese attack somewhere in the Pacific. He placed it carefully in his bag.

Moments later, he pedaled off to Navy headquarters, eight miles away.

It was a thirty-minute ride.

PART 2

CHAPTER 6

I̲t̲ ̲w̲a̲s̲ ̲a̲ ̲q̲u̲i̲e̲t̲ ̲m̲o̲r̲n̲i̲n̲g̲ ̲o̲n̲ ̲O̲a̲h̲u̲.

Joe Lockard and George Elliott, both Army privates, manned the isolated post that Sunday. Three men normally pulled duty at Opana Radar Station, but one had decided to sleep in.

Lockard was nineteen years old, just barely out of high school in Williamsport, Pennsylvania. He liked to tinker and also painted and wrote poetry. When he joined the Army a few months earlier, going to war was the furthest thing from his mind. "It was a tropical post," he recalled. "It was peacetime. It was a nice place to have a tour of duty."

Opana had been operating only since Thanksgiving, and Lockard had received almost no instruction on the job. Private Elliott knew even less. This wasn't exactly a sought-after assignment; one radar man commented that "if you got into trouble in the Army, a radar unit was most likely in your future."

A pickup truck dropped them at the camp at the beginning of their shift and retrieved them afterward, working its way slowly up and down a rutted dirt road.

The station was little more than a tall antenna and a few parked trucks filled with radar equipment. Thanks to its location at Kahuku Point, the radar had a range of 150 miles. At more than five hundred feet high, the hilltop offered sweeping views of sparkling blue waters reaching out to the horizon.

It was, the US Army assumed, the ideal spot to detect an enemy approaching from the sea.

Five such radar sites ringed the island of Oahu, all of them connected by telephone to a control center in Fort Shafter, which could alert the Army Air Forces at Wheeler Field to the presence of any incoming enemy planes. The telephone connection wasn't always reliable, and one station had been advised by the higher-ups to use a local gas station's pay phone to call in any reports of activity.

Only one radar site was in operation that morning— manned by two inexperienced Army privates.

Private Joseph Lockard manning the
radar station at Opana, in an undated photograph.

They'd been up since four AM.

Lockard and Elliott took turns on the equipment:
One watched the gray screen of the oscilloscope—a
boxy device that looked like an early version of a tele-
vision set—while the other plotted the location of any
aircraft picked up by the radar.

But Lockard found that the set operated inconsis-
tently. "It was possible to pick up one plane...and it was
also sometimes *im*possible to pick up three or four," he
recalled.

Normally, the presence of an aircraft out over the sea would produce echoes, which appeared as white pulses on the face of the oscilloscope. Except this morning, there weren't any aircraft at all, and the screen was blank.

At six forty-five, the radar screen flickered—and then went dark again. And then, just before seven, a call came in from Fort Shafter: It was time to shut the station down and go back to base camp.

As usual, the pickup truck was late, and there was only one way down the mountain, so waiting was Lockard and Elliott's only option.

Elliott sorely needed practice on the radar machine, and he was happy to let it go on for a while. With Lockard looking over his shoulder, he switched on the oscilloscope and watched for the telltale white blips on the screen.

Nothing appeared at first, but at 7:02, the screen lit up with white pulses.

The men had never seen so many aircraft. Lockard quickly switched places with Elliott and took over the set. "I fooled around some more," he recalled, "trying to determine exactly whether it was something coming in or whether it was a defect in the equipment, and finally decided that it was a flight of some sort."

Elliott plotted the incoming planes on a physical

chart. Whatever was out there was creeping closer and closer to the coast, minute by minute.

"Call the information center and see if there is anyone around," Lockard said to Elliott.

But when Elliott reached Private Joseph McDonald, the switchboard operator at the radar information center at Fort Shafter, the man told him the center was empty.

By now, Elliott was panicking at the thought of what might be headed their way and told McDonald about the large number of radar blips on his screen. Sensing Elliott's anxiety, McDonald immediately rang off and went to look for someone. He came across Lieutenant Kermit Tyler, seated alone at a plotting table. Everyone else had gone to breakfast. McDonald told Tyler about the unusual radar reading at Opana.

After only a few weeks at this post, Lieutenant Tyler had even less experience than Lockard or Elliott. His commanding officers had given him no reason to sound the alarm about unidentified aircraft—in fact, no one had told him much of anything about what his assignment *was* at Ford Shafter.

Tyler decided there was no reason for alarm, but McDonald persuaded him to call back the men at Opana anyway.

Lockard picked up this time. "I have never seen anything like this," he told Tyler.

Tyler paused for a moment to think about it. Finally, he offered Lockard the most sensible explanation he could come up with. "You see," Tyler said, "I had a friend who was a bomber pilot, and he told me any time that they play this Hawaiian music all night long, it is a very good indication that our B-17s were coming over from the mainland, because they use it for homing."

Hawaiian music had been playing all night on the local radio. And, in fact, there really was a group of B-17 bombers due to land on Oahu that morning. If Lockard had detected something on his oscilloscope, it was probably just that same squadron.

"Don't worry about it," Tyler said to Lockard, and hung up.

Just then, a few minutes past seven thirty, the truck arrived at the radar station to pick them up. Lockard and Elliott turned off the radar, locked the station, and headed back down the hill.

———◇———

Mitsuo Fuchida switched on the radio of his Nakajima B5N bomber and turned the dial until he heard luau music playing in his headset. By adjusting the antenna on his instrument panel and listening carefully to the volume of the broadcast, he could determine precisely where the signal was beaming in from. As he did so, the daily weather report from the Honolulu station KGMB tuned in. Using the radio signal as a guide, he changed course, steering his plane directly toward Pearl Harbor.

Soaring behind Fuchida in his dive-bomber, pilot Zenji Abe craned his neck impatiently, trying to catch a glimpse of something, anything, through the clouds. What would Pearl Harbor look like? Would the maps he had studied so carefully lead them to their target?

"Finally," he recalled, "a white line appeared, breaking the smooth edge where water meets the sky. Above the white line of the breakers was a blue-violet color. 'There is Oahu,' I informed Saito [his navigator] through the voice tube, trying to keep my voice calm. I approached the island with a mixture of dreadful fear and fascination. I felt it was the 'devil's island' of Japanese legend."

After months of preparation and an exhausting journey across the Pacific Ocean, this was the moment of truth. Everything—their entire battle plan—depended on the element of surprise. Fuchida instructed his copilot to keep a lookout for enemy planes, but as the seconds passed and the lush green landscape of Oahu passed beneath him, none appeared.

They had traveled *four thousand miles* without being detected by the enemy.

At 7:49, Fuchida shouted into his intercom, signaling to the attacking Japanese planes that their surprise was complete, using the code word they had prepared in advance.

"*Tora! Tora! Tora!*" "Tiger! Tiger! Tiger!"

Fuchida slid open his canopy and fired a single flare, a sign to his fellow pilots to commence their attack on Pearl Harbor.

———◇———

The rumble of aircraft woke up an unsuspecting family several thousand feet below, in their beach house in Haleiwa, on Oahu's north shore. Their dogs barked furiously at the noise overhead. James Mann and his son stepped outside to see for themselves what the fuss was about—surely, they thought, an early-morning Navy drill.

Hundreds of planes of all sizes soared over the house, glinting in the sun, streaming inland toward the far side of the island.

Puzzled at the sight, thirteen-year-old Junior Mann pointed upward. Kids his age on Oahu had grown accustomed to Navy drills and to the thrill of watching aerial maneuvers. A boy like Junior usually had no trouble telling one fighter plane from another, but these were unfamiliar to him.

Like nearly all the Americans who witnessed the first wave of Mitsuo Fuchida's squadrons that morning, Junior came up with an explanation that seemed to make sense out of what he was seeing.

"They've changed the color of our planes!" he said.

At the opposite end of Oahu, nine-year-old Arthur Uchida was up early that morning, playing in his yard in Alewa Heights, a leafy neighborhood overlooking the city of Honolulu.

Arthur and his neighborhood friends played war games that morning, gripping wooden guns they made themselves. They raced around his yard, taking aim at one another. Calling a truce, Arthur planted a white flag on the lawn, and it fluttered in the morning breeze as the sun rose over Oahu in the east.

Just before eight, as the sounds of airplanes droned over the distant hills, his mother called him inside for breakfast.

—◇—

The first wave of the Japanese attack, with Fuchida in the lead, broke into different groups, according to plan. Each group traced a different path over the green hills of Oahu and the blue water surrounding it, following routes they had memorized. They flew low to avoid detection by the American military forces.

An attack group of dive-bombers and Zero fighters swooped over the hills above Honolulu (and Arthur Uchida's house), then bore down toward Operation Z's first target: the massive naval airfields on Ford Island, where hundreds of aircraft sat out in the open, fully exposed to the mayhem coming their way.

They descended quickly toward the flat, oblong island in the middle of Pearl Harbor.

CHAPTER 7

MARY ANN RAMSEY WAS STARTLED AWAKE BY A phone ringing and an unfamiliar tone in her father's voice: fear.

"Are you sure, Dick? All right. I'll be down immediately!"

Her father, Logan Ramsey, got off the emergency phone call from Admiral Bellinger's office and dashed down the hallway. Mary Ann Ramsey's last glimpse of him was in his Hawaiian shirt, rushing out the front door.

Moments later, the distinctive whine of airplane engines filled the room.

When the first bombs fell on Ford Island, the sound reached her first, their sharp concussions passing through her body. The fireballs came next, leaving behind black craters mere yards from their home.

The Ramsey house, like many tropical structures, had wooden walls and no basement. Mary knew they had to get out of there.

But now she faced two problems: Her father had left her alone with her mother, and her mother was sitting up in bed, immobilized by fear.

It was up to Mary to get her mother to safety. She remembered that Admiral Bellinger's nearby home was built over an old ammunition depot; would that protect them from the explosions? It was across open ground, just a short distance away. The only way to get there was to run.

As Mary pulled her mother out the front door, a squadron of Japanese torpedo bombers—having just swooped in and finished a bombing run—passed directly over the Ramseys' house. Mary was already on the move when something, probably a piece of flying shrapnel, ricocheted off her metal bracelet—a gift from her dad from his recent trip to the island of Nouméa. When she glanced down at her wrist, a gap now marred the design.

She kept running through the chaos and smoke. The distance to the Bellingers' house seemed endless.

They made it to the underground shelter at last—and found terrified civilians already cowering there.

One woman knelt in the corner, quietly praying while fingering her rosary beads. A newborn baby's screams filled the cramped space. Everyone seemed stunned and speechless by a world turned upside down.

Above them, the bombs kept coming. One landed so close that it shook the shelter like an earthquake.

"The entire island seemed to be blowing up," Mary said.

——◇——

Just before eight in the morning, sailors on the battleship *Oklahoma*'s main deck saw puffs of smoke in the distance as the first Japanese bombs struck Ford Island just beyond Battleship Row, where the enormous *Oklahoma* was moored. Confused shouts echoed across the ship. Belowdecks, sailors who had been relaxing over coffee sat up straight.

"What is this? Drills on a Sunday?"

"What the hell is going on?"

Moments later, the men spied a group of planes flying low, aiming directly for the battleship. With each passing second, the aircraft seemed to grow larger and larger. The Navy's own fliers must be simulating an attack, one man guessed.

What the sailors on the *Oklahoma* were witnessing made no sense to them. Those had to be American planes. Pearl Harbor sat thousands of miles from anything; who else could they be? But why would they be using live ammunition on a Sunday, and so close to the fleet?

Nineteen-year-old Herbert Kennedy heard what sounded like popping noises. Machine gun bullets whined overhead, ricocheting across the *Oklahoma*.

Kennedy couldn't believe his eyes as the first bullets struck the ship. The sailor across from him was struck down. "Blood spattered all over me," Kennedy recalled, "and I didn't know what to think."

Fifteen-year-old Martin Matthews had spent the night aboard the nearby *Arizona* on December 6, visiting a friend. Just two months earlier, he had snuck into the Navy by forging his enlistment papers, claiming to be two years older. Matthews was hungry for adventure. He woke early on the morning of December 7 because he was excited about touring the famous battleship.

Martin was standing on the ship's open deck a few minutes after eight that morning when he heard noises in the distance. Planes, swooping low over the water, seemed to be heading toward him—but planes were nothing unusual in Pearl Harbor, where Navy pilots constantly drilled and maneuvered in the skies above.

Behind the planes, thunder boomed in the distance. Martin didn't know that the noise was actually bombs striking Ford Island—the sounds traveled faster than news of the Japanese attack.

"None of us thought about bombs," Martin said. "We didn't know what a bomb was yet; I had never seen one in my life."

The first squadrons of Japanese planes opened fire mercilessly on the big ships after their first pass over Hickam Field. Thousands of bullets and aerial bombs broke over Battleship Row in a wave of fire and steel, shattering the safety and calm. On the open decks, men dived for cover, desperate to stay alive. Inside, hundreds more woke to the muffled sounds of the battle outside.

These were boys and men who had never seen combat, and their senses recoiled at the sharp crack of gunfire and the heavy thump of bombs striking the earth and water. For the first few seconds, most of the Americans on the ground and on the ships moored in the water could only watch as the first Japanese planes sliced through the air overhead. And then, like swimmers who finally reach the surface, they gasped at the terror coming out of the sky.

———◇———

Smoke was the first thing Ernest Reid noticed as his unarmed B-17 bomber approached Pearl Harbor from the east. Reid's navigator figured that a nearby sugar plantation's workers must be burning cane fields after the harvest, to clear them for the next growing season.

After fourteen hours in the air, the crews were exhausted. By an accident of timing, the American bombers flew right into the first wave of the Japanese attack on Pearl Harbor, at the precise moment that the first Japanese fighters were dropping their deadly payloads on the unsuspecting Americans below.

The crew lowered the bomber's landing gear and flaps just as Hickam's main runway came into view. The sight below them was almost incomprehensible: Six American fighter planes were fully engulfed in flames on the tarmac, sending black clouds billowing.

As the recognition sank in, a hail of bullets ripped through Reid's aircraft, sparking a fire. A crew member cried out, his leg streaming with blood. Only a few hundred feet off the ground, Reid struggled to keep the big aircraft on course, aiming straight for the runway as smoke filled the cabin and flames licked at his back.

"As we hit the ground," Reid recalled, "the fire was so intense that the plane literally buckled in two."

The B-17 skidded to a halt. Thanks to Reid's skillful piloting, the crew, though battered and shot up, were still alive. They leaped from the wreckage, helping the wounded, and scattered in all directions. The B-17 had

PHOTOGRAPHER UNKNOWN. US NATIONAL ARCHIVES AND RECORDS ADMINISTRATION PHOTOGRAPH, DECEMBER 7, 1941.

A partially destroyed B-17, one of the squadron that landed amid the Japanese attack, sits on the tarmac of Hickam Field.

been struck by three Japanese Zero fighters, and those same three planes now banked sharply. They were strafing the airfield—aiming directly at the American flight crews as they ran for cover.

Reid and two other men sprinted across a clearing toward a group of houses in the distance. They made it just as the Japanese bullets chewed up the runway.

Only steps from the mayhem of Hickam Field, neat rows of officers' houses with manicured gardens stood untouched. The attack had come so quickly that some of its residents were only now waking up to the shocking reality.

Reid ducked into the entryway of a home and knocked on the door. A woman who appeared to be a maid answered, her face a picture of surprise at the filthy and injured crew.

"Who is it, Marie?" a voice called from inside the house.

"There's some men here," the maid answered, "and I think they've been hurt."

———◇———

The Western Union bicycle messenger carrying the warning from General Marshall was still pedaling when the first bombs struck the US fleet; his message never reached Navy headquarters.

Admiral Kimmel, the commander of the US Pacific Fleet, was getting dressed that morning inside his house some distance from Pearl Harbor. Just after eight his telephone rang.

It was the admiral's aide. "There's a message from the signal tower saying the Japanese are attacking Pearl Harbor and this is no drill," he said.

Kimmel hurried outside to his front lawn, which had a view of the base in the distance. He could clearly see Japanese planes circling above Battleship Row, which was already enveloped in smoke.

A neighbor stood next to the admiral, watching in astonishment. When she looked over at Kimmel, she noticed that his face "was as white as the uniform he wore."

CHAPTER 8

WHILE FUCHIDA'S DIVE-BOMBERS AND FIGHTERS HARASSED the Americans over Ford Island, twenty-four Japanese torpedo bombers soared in from the west in a single, disciplined line, each plane separated from the next by only several hundred yards—and each carrying a two-thousand-pound torpedo. Their sole mission was to sink American ships.

Pilot Jinichi Goto gripped the controls, swooping down from the dark green Oahu hills. He steered his torpedo plane toward the USS *Oklahoma* in the dangerous, low-altitude approach that he and his fellow pilots had practiced again and again in the seas around Japan.

He descended quickly, practically skimming the waters of Pearl Harbor. The long glass canopy of Goto's aircraft gave its three-man crew a clear view of the huge American naval base.

Already the scene beneath them was turning chaotic as smoke and flames rose from Ford Island. "The hangars were aflame and the planes on the ground were burning," pilot Yuji Akamatsu recalled. "I saw American soldiers pulling hoses and riding bicycles and trying to put out the fires."

When the Japanese pilots crossed over the harbor, the ships they had studied for hours on end—using photos taken by the spy Morimura—seemed like phantoms. "It now seemed hard to believe," pilot Juzo Mori thought, "that we were actually here to sink them."

The time had come to bring glory to Japan. "In a few hours," Mori reflected, "the attack would be headline news in every corner of the globe and people around the world would be in awe at our stupendous victory."

In the final moments of the attack sequence, Mori brought his plane to within mere feet of the harbor's surface. The weight of the torpedo pulled him downward, and Mori could feel and hear the strain of the engine. He glanced at his altimeter, which read nearly zero: His bomber was soaring no more than a couple of feet above the flat water.

He took deep breaths to calm himself, clearing his mind of all distractions.

Moments later, the row of battleships rose up in front of him. "If they had placed torpedo nets on their exposed sides," Mori said, "we could never have torpedoed them."

Maneuvering his own aircraft just behind Mori's, Jinichi Goto pulled a handle that released his torpedo, dropping it into the water. He banked sharply after the launch, veering so close to the *Oklahoma* that he soared past the crow's nest on one of the enormous ship's central towers. As he steered upward into the sky, his co-pilot observed a waterspout exploding in front of the ship.

"Ararimashita!" "It struck!" he cried into his radio.

Now it was Mori's turn, and he bore down on the familiar outline of the USS *California*, which he recognized from hours of careful study in Japan.

"I felt the plane leap skywards as the heavy torpedo dropped away," he recalled. "As I zoomed over the ship I could see the American sailors staring up at us. It seemed like they still didn't realize they were being attacked."

He craned his neck backward just in time to see another enormous waterspout as his thunderfish slammed directly into the *California*'s exposed hull.

PHOTOGRAPHER UNKNOWN. US NAVY, NAVAL HISTORY AND HERITAGE COMMAND PHOTOGRAPHY COLLECTION, DECEMBER 7, 1941.

American sailors look on as smoke rises from the USS *California* (*left*) and *Oklahoma* (*right*), moments after being struck by the first Japanese torpedoes.

———◇———

A sailor aboard the battleship *West Virginia*, just a few hundred feet in front of the *Oklahoma*, was tracking two Japanese planes flying low over the harbor when he spied two objects drop from the aircraft, then splash as they landed in the water. "Suddenly I spotted two wakes heading for the ship," he said. "By the time I got the word *torpedoes* out of my mouth, they had hit and exploded."

At about the same time, another sailor stood on the

open deck of the *Oklahoma* and watched as a Japanese torpedo bomber arced steeply upward after dropping his deadly payload. The pilot flew so close to the ship that the sailor made eye contact with him.

The *Oklahoma* shook twice, violently. The exploding torpedoes sent great fountains of water and debris shooting a thousand feet into the air. After a moment's pause, tons of water came crashing back down onto the ship, forcing men to their knees as it swamped the decks.

Inside the *Oklahoma*, nobody had any warning of the torpedo strikes.

Adolph Mortensen had been sleeping in his bunk when the first alarms sounded. It was hot that night

PHOTOGRAPHER UNKNOWN. US NATIONAL ARCHIVES AND RECORDS ADMINISTRATION PHOTOGRAPHY COLLECTION.

A photo taken by a Japanese pilot shows the huge waterspout that followed a torpedo strike against the USS *West Virginia*. The exploding torpedo sent tons of water shooting into the air.

belowdecks and he and his bunkmate slept with the portholes open to let some air in. Mortensen wore pajama bottoms—and little else—as he leaped into action, pausing only to put on a cap and slippers. His bunkmate was only steps ahead of him.

"We did not see one another again for six months," he said.

Mortensen's battle station was forward and below, in the ship's boiler control room. He hurried through narrow passageways, past staterooms and abandoned Army cots whose occupants had rushed to their own stations moments earlier.

The Japanese torpedoes traveled at over sixty miles per hour underwater. When they struck, the explosions sent massive shock waves through the entire structure of the battleship. Each time, the Oklahoma shuddered. Officers ordered the crew to retreat belowdecks, where—they believed—the men would be safe from the attack.

Nearly fourteen hundred sailors grabbed hold of whatever they could and struggled to stay upright in the cramped spaces. Mortensen's legs buckled with each blast, and he stumbled over loose equipment and dodged unhinged berths. In the mess hall, he slipped on floors covered with that day's breakfast and coffee, mixed with baloney and tomato sauce.

The *Oklahoma* was built to survive an attack like this. The Japanese pilots had done their work, but the ship seemed to hold steady.

Was the worst over?

———◇———

Minutes after the first two torpedoes struck the battleship *Oklahoma*, a third thunderfish finally penetrated the battleship's supposedly torpedo-proof hull. The shock of that impact was followed by an explosion that sent water and diesel oil cascading across the ship's wooden decks.

Almost imperceptibly at first, but then more and more, the huge ship listed to the side.

The unimaginable was happening as seawater poured into the ship's passages through a gaping hole. In mere seconds, the six-hundred-foot *Oklahoma* began to tilt toward the water line as the weight of the water pulled it over on its side.

Belowdecks, the sights were even more surreal, as men who had only just reached their battle stations suddenly found their orderly world upside down. In the crowded compartments, men and equipment slid along the walls, and sailors braced their feet on the ceiling. Confused shouts and garbled orders were drowned out by the deafening clang of metal pans, furniture, and equipment ricocheting off steel beams and heavy bulkheads.

The *Oklahoma* rotated sideways into the water, coming to rest only when its tall conning tower struck the muddy bottom of Pearl Harbor. Like a giant beached whale, the ship's black hull now rested above water, exposed to the air. It was an otherworldly sight. No boat of this size had ever "turned turtle" on the water—and few people alive had seen the upturned hull of an American battleship.

———◇———

"We're trapped," Stephen Bower Young said out loud. Only a day before, he had been enjoying Oahu's sunny weather; now he couldn't see through the darkness inside the upside-down ship.

The *Oklahoma*'s sudden rotation had created not only scenes of havoc but also pockets of air throughout the ship's warren of rooms—for those lucky enough to find them in the pitch dark.

Young was among the lucky. "I surfaced," he recalled, "gulped for air, and automatically began to swim, or more exactly to tread water, in the confining space of the handling room."

Other voices pierced the darkness, and Young realized he was not alone. Some shined flashlights, the beams of light darting off the murky and rising waters.

"Here, over here," someone yelled.

Survivors gathered, then felt their way into a nearby storage room. The water hadn't risen completely here, and they clambered up the bulkheads, grabbing hold of anything they could.

The air pocket was large enough. But with so many sets of lungs breathing in and out, the oxygen could last for only so long.

"We had to do something, anything, to get out of here," Young thought.

CHAPTER 9

ONE BY ONE, THE JAPANESE TORPEDO BOMBERS descended from the sky, taking aim at Battleship Row. In under ten minutes, the most fearsome weapons in America's military arsenal appeared to be losing the battle against a single squadron of lightly armored aircraft in the hands of Japan's finest pilots.

The great battleships were sitting ducks, completely exposed and unable to escape the next strike.

The repair ship USS *Vestal* was anchored alongside the *Arizona*, lashed to the warship so that work crews could begin repairs that morning on its portholes. On the *Vestal*, a deckhand gazed out at a Japanese plane barreling over the water. He stood motionless as the plane dropped its torpedo into the harbor. "You could see the wake of the torpedo and it looked like it was coming to you," he said, describing the frothy white line that traveled like an underwater arrow toward the ship.

The *Vestal*'s shallow hull saved it that day: The torpedo passed right underneath it, slamming instead at full speed into the massive steel hull of the *Arizona*.

A muffled boom echoed deep within the bowels of the battleship, reverberating like a bass drum. The ship was so large that not everyone inside understood what had happened; some assumed that men from the *Vestal* had begun their repair work early and that they were simply hearing the noisy air hammers and other tools.

Private First Class James Cory was close enough to feel the terrifying impact of the Japanese torpedo. "You could feel the decks—the compartments—being penetrated just like you could hold a taut piece of cloth or two or three pieces separated by your fingers and feel a needle go through them," he recalled. "That's the way it felt."

Men started running as general quarters—the alert that sent sailors to their battle stations—was sounded throughout the ship. Martin Matthews was left standing all alone amid the pandemonium, with no idea at all where to go. He just stood in the back of the ship's decks, not moving, a child in the middle of a mechanized war.

"I was petrified," he said. "To put it in plain English, it scared the living hell out of me."

Unlike the *Oklahoma*, however, the *Arizona* survived this first strike, battered but still seaworthy. Perhaps some of the American fleet could withstand Japan's torpedoes after all.

———◇———

Moments later, a different threat appeared in the skies, high overhead.

Flying ten thousand feet above Pearl Harbor, an attack squadron of Japanese heavy bombers spotted the distinctive line of ships on Battleship Row, far beneath them. They used specially calibrated bombsights to home in on their approaching targets with extreme accuracy.

One after another, their high-explosive bombs tumbled out of the sky.

Within seconds, the bombs found their mark, striking the forward decks of the *Arizona*. They wreaked havoc on the thick wooden planks, blowing shards in all directions and scattering the men unlucky enough to find themselves out in the open.

Martin Matthews watched as more bombs rained

down, making their way closer and closer to where he stood.

"I was trying to get under cover," he recalled, "but at my age and not prepared for this, I was scared to death.... I was too damned young to realize what was going on. I didn't even know that this was a war breaking out. I just thought this was some big mistake that was being made."

With nowhere to run, Martin turned and dived over the ship's railing, tumbling toward the water below. When he came up for air, he spotted a barnacle-crusted buoy in the distance and swam toward it.

———◆———

The *Arizona* was a war machine built for victory on the high seas. Its thick hull and powerful guns could destroy smaller ships and pound the enemy from safe distances. But on this morning, bearing down on the battleship's exposed wooden decks, the Japanese pilots found the *Arizona*'s soft spot.

Three bull's-eyes rocked the big ship hard. And at 8:08 AM, a fourth bomb penetrated the *Arizona*'s wooden deck and exploded below, sparking a fire in the ship's heavily packed ammunition magazine.

ATTACKED!

A millisecond later, a blast with the force of over a million pounds of gunpowder sent a massive, invisible wave of energy traveling outward, faster than the speed of sound.

In a Navy administration building on Ford Island, the concrete floor rippled. One man reported feeling as if he had been squeezed tightly, then released.

High in the air over Oahu, several miles from the *Arizona*, Mitsuo Fuchida's plane shook as the blast wave passed through it.

The USS *Arizona* detonates after being struck by a Japanese bomb.

The explosion lifted the mighty *Arizona* into the air, thirty thousand tons of steel and wood. Just as quickly, the big ship crashed back into the water and cracked in half.

Clinging to his buoy, Martin Matthews watched as the massive blast's fallout rained down onto Pearl Harbor. "I remember lots of steel and bodies coming down," he said. "I saw a thigh and leg; I saw fingers; I saw hands; I saw elbows and arms. It's far too much for a young boy of fifteen to have seen."

Though covered with black oil, Martin himself escaped without a scratch.

———◇———

On what was left of the ship, time seemed to unfold in slow motion for the few men who survived, their ears ringing and skin seared by the heat.

"The ship had become a piece of molten steel, a kind of giant tea kettle," one sailor remembered. He saw wounded men everywhere, wailing in pain. Another watched powerlessly as his friend cried for help. "His skin was hanging off him," the man said. "There was nothing in the world I could do for him."

James Cory climbed down twisted ladders, trying not to touch the searing-hot railings. When he finally reached the blazing deck, he came face-to-face with a horrifying sight.

"There were bodies of men," Cory said. "These people were zombies, in essence. They were burned completely white. Their skin was just as white as if you'd taken a bucket of whitewash and painted it white. Their hair was burned off; their eyebrows were burned off; the pitiful remnants of their uniforms in their crotch was a charred remnant; and the insoles of their shoes was about the only thing that was left on these bodies. They were moving like robots. Their arms were out, held away from their bodies, and they were stumping along the decks. These were burned men!"

For the survivors on the *Arizona*, no hope remained.

An injured sailor named John Rampley had to crawl across the deck of the burning battleship. All he could see was wreckage ahead of him, metal twisted in every direction. He spied a raft on the harbor below; men were scrambling to pull themselves onto it. Just then, another Japanese plane descended toward the ship, machine guns blazing. In desperation, Rampley leaped into the water and began to swim toward Ford Island.

With Japanese planes still overhead, the waters of Pearl Harbor offered safety from the burning *Arizona*—but little else. The explosion had spilled thousands of gallons of fuel oil into the harbor, where it floated on the surface. "People who have never seen this at sea cannot imagine what oil is like once it is exposed to cool seawater," Rampley said. "It becomes a globlike carpet about six inches thick, gelatinous."

Men thrashed about in the oily froth, looking for anything solid to cling to. But the floating fuel then became a lethal weapon as the roaring flames from the ship showered sparks onto it, igniting it all at once.

Fire rose on the water around the *Arizona*, engulfing many of the few survivors who had made it off the ship. Some disappeared. Others, alone or in small, desperate groups, found paths through the flames, paddling away from the burning wreck toward dry land.

"The most vivid recording in my memory bank of that ordeal," an *Arizona* sailor recalled, "was the hundreds of white sailors' hats floating in the salty brine, with their black stenciled names in full view."

Fire engulfs the ships of Battleship Row
as a rescue boat crew looks on.

Nine minutes after a Japanese bomb crashed through its decks, the *Arizona* sank to the bottom of Pearl Harbor, carrying with it 1,177 victims—the most lethal single attack in all American history at that point.

As the huge battleship settled on the silty bottom, what was left of the survivors' sense of safety disappeared with it. Swimming for their lives, trapped in the *Oklahoma*'s hull, running for safety on Ford Island and

Hickam Field—the Americans of Pearl Harbor had seen their world turned on its head.

Like millions of their fellow citizens, they had believed that war would never come to American shores. In the space of thirty minutes, that fantasy had become a nightmare.

CHAPTER 10

A RATTLING SOUND WOKE DONALD KELI'INOI. THE windowpanes in his room were shaking in the frames. He was trying to figure out why when his dad rushed into the bedroom. "Hey," he hollered, "we got something going on out there." Donald leaped out of bed and ran onto the front porch of his small home, overlooking the Keli'inoi farm on the other side of Pearl Harbor.

Overhead, an American plane seemed to fly straight up, and then exploded into a fireball as a Japanese fighter peppered it with bullets. The fighter then made a huge arc in the sky, and the whole family watched in amazement until it became clear that it was headed their way.

The impact of bullets hitting their front yard reached them before the sound. "It was as if someone took a pick and dug up our front yard—the dirt was bouncing up." Donald's father collared his family and rushed them inside.

Inside, the whole Keli'inoi family lingered nervously, afraid of what might happen next in a place where nothing much had happened before. They felt alone. "We were so far out in the boonies," Donald said, "that nobody even knew we existed."

War had come to Pu'uloa Farms, tearing up the earth, bringing fire and steel to the skies overhead. It was so sudden that Donald might still have been dreaming—but his real life was about to change forever.

———◇———

To outsiders, the Damon Tract neighborhood seemed like a shantytown of shoulder-to-shoulder, hastily built houses. But to its residents, it was a place alive at all hours with the comings and goings of plantation workers, pungent smells rising from hundreds of kitchens, chickens clucking, and the rising and falling of voices in English and Tagalog.

Nine-year-old Alfredo Fernandez and his three siblings trudged to eight o'clock mass at Saint Philomena that Sunday. The little Catholic church sat on T Road, just a short walk from the Fernandez home in Damon Tract. The priests and nuns of Saint Philomena ministered to the large Filipino community that lived in the tight grid of streets just to the east of Hickam Field.

But this morning, unfamiliar sounds bounced off the walls of the neighborhood's densely packed streets.

"As soon as we got out of the house," Alfredo recalled, "we heard a loud *boom* here and a *boom* there, you know, then we heard *rat-tat-tat-tat-tat*."

As the kids walked down the middle of the road toward church, a Japanese plane rocketed over them, flying so low that they could see the pilot and the red circle on the fuselage. Still, like nearly everyone else that morning, the children assumed that they were watching a training maneuver—a very realistic one.

A cloud of black smoke rose in the distance as the children arrived at Saint Philomena. Inside, the priest proceeded with the church service nervously as the whistling of antiaircraft shells and the rapid pops of machine gun fire grew louder outside. Alfredo could even hear the ping of shrapnel shards landing on the roof and the street.

In Damon Tract, on the streets of Honolulu, and in the hills above the city, news of the Japanese attack literally fell out of the sky. Bullets and exploding shells crashed through roofs, tore up pavement, and shattered windowpanes, proving that this was no drill. The Japanese seemed to have the whole island in their sights, targeting battleships and apartment blocks with equal fury.

It was only later that civilians began to realize that they had been the victims of "friendly fire" from the

A civilian car on a road in Oahu, damaged by stray American antiaircraft fire on the morning of December 7, 1941. The driver and two passengers, three members of the same family, died in the accident.

wild firing of .50-caliber machine guns and antiaircraft artillery by the Americans themselves.

A stray artillery shell, probably fired from an American ship, obliterated the Cherry Blossom Restaurant in Honolulu. Twelve people, including a father and his three children, died in the explosion. Janet Yumiko Ohta was killed at home, along with her mother and her aunt, when an antiaircraft round struck them.

In all, forty-nine civilians died that morning, the youngest just three months old.

———◇———

While whole families dashed for cover on the ground, in the skies overhead almost unbelievable scenes of war unfolded.

"We actually saw planes dive-bombing," Alfredo said. "We saw them go down out of sight, then shoot up again. Then a few seconds later we would hear this loud *boom*. Then we'd see this billowing black smoke."

When the skies cleared briefly, Alfred and his siblings joined a stream of almost a thousand people hurrying out of the heavily populated neighborhood. They followed the railroad tracks, heading in the direction of the city. Alfred saw adults carrying pillowcases stuffed with their belongings.

Police and soldiers seemed to be everywhere in their olive-drab uniforms, herding families. They wore stern expressions on their faces. Some carried rifles with sharp-tipped bayonets—as if the Filipinos of Damon Tract were threatening Oahu as much as the Japanese pilots soaring above them.

Rumors of a possible Japanese invasion swept through the white population of Honolulu. They had always eyed the island's Asian immigrant populations suspiciously, seeing them as potential saboteurs and possible traitors. But now those suspicions burst into full view. As the Japanese bore down from the skies, some people in Hawaii were already drawing new lines on the ground. Who was an enemy, who was an ally?

———◇———

Kimiko Watanabe startled awake at home that morning with her infant son, Dickie, beside her. She shared a bed with him in her little apartment on Kukui Street, her arm cradled around the baby boy. It was her way of keeping him safe during the long stretches of time when her husband, Kiho, was out at sea on his fishing boat, the *Kiho Maru*.

Kiho promised Kimiko that this would be his last trip. He wanted to work on land, to wake each morning with his family and not bobbing on the Pacific Ocean, in a sampan reeking of fish.

Though only twenty, Kimiko had spent much of her young life working: on pineapple plantations, as a maid in the homes of white people, and in the big laundry at the Navy's Schofield Barracks, pressing pants and shirts from morning till night. Now, though, Kiho's earnings from fishing allowed her to stay home for the first time in her life. She was safe and happy.

Kimiko's bedroom window offered a fine view across the city to Pearl Harbor. She sat up suddenly and puzzled over the sight of bombs exploding where there was usually nothing but pristine blue-green water. Just then her uncle knocked on the door: Kimiko had no radio or telephone, and he had come to bring her news.

"Oh Kimiko," he said, "over there *senseo natta itte kara*. Pearl Harbor attack *shittate*. Kiho *mada modoran ka itte*?" "Oh Kimiko, over there, war started, Pearl Harbor was attacked. Hasn't Kiho returned yet?"

Plumes of black smoke unfurled above the harbor. From a distance, the engines of the Japanese planes sounded like hornets, buzzing and whining across the sky.

"No," Kimiko said.

Modotte kuru no, she thought, trying to reassure herself. They would return.

———◇———

Like the diesel oil oozing across the surface of Pearl Harbor, a dark, unfamiliar fear seeped beyond the morning's military targets and into the homes and bedrooms of thousands of civilians—children, teenagers, men and women, many of whom were waking to what they assumed would be an ordinary day. They were accustomed to seeing ships, planes, and soldiers everywhere they went, but for that very reason, it had felt like war could be kept at bay forever.

Pearl Harbor, until that very moment, had made them feel safe. Now danger seemed to be coming at them from all directions.

PART 3

CHAPTER 11

THE FIRST WAVE OF SURVIVORS FROM BATTLESHIP ROW trudged out of the water coated in a thick layer of oil.

Hundreds of men huddled in a long, six-foot-wide irrigation trench on Ford Island, wet and shivering, unsure of going forward into the unknown and terrified of going back into the water. Other dazed and injured men wandered into the open grass, calling for help while Japanese fighters still strafed and bombed them from above.

Those who could run raced across the exposed clearings, seeking safety in barracks and other nearby buildings. Smoke choked their lungs. Cordite pellets, tiny kernels of explosives that had been stored deep in the hold of the *Arizona*, rained down from the sky like a black hailstorm.

In the Navy headquarters building, officers and enlisted men rigged up makeshift first-aid stations while others scoured the rooms for towels, blankets, and spare clothing. Sailors hauled mattresses onto the floor of the mess hall for the wounded and tore sheets from beds to wipe the oil off survivors. One officer went from window to window, smashing the glass with a golf club to prevent flying shards from injuring men when the bombs exploded outside. Another located a stock of morphine and helped administer shots of the pain-killer to the most seriously injured and burned. To make sure that nobody was accidentally given a fatal second dose, he dabbed their foreheads with Mercurochrome, an antiseptic liquid that stains the skin.

Lieutenant Elmer Schuessler, a veteran of the Army Medical Service in World War I, sprinted across open ground in search of medical supplies as bullets ate up the pavement and bombs detonated all around him.

Nearby, in the air-raid shelter beneath Admiral Bellinger's house, Mary Ann Ramsey heard a commotion outside.

"A young man, filthy black oil covering his burned, shredded flesh, walked in unaided," she recalled. "He had no clothes on, his nudity entirely obscured by oil.

The skin hung from his arms like scarlet ribbons as he staggered toward my mother for help."

The man looked at Mary Ann and touched his throat, unable to speak; she guessed that he had swallowed some of the oil as he swam from a ship to Ford Island.

More men followed, crowding into the cramped space as Japanese bombs shook the ground overhead.

No one seemed in charge—and no one had thought to store medicine or first-aid supplies in the bunker. So Mary Ann, a sixteen-year-old young woman among dozens of severely injured sailors and terrified adults, gathered up her courage and started moving carefully among the casualties. She offered them water. She held cigarettes for men who could not use their hands, to help calm their frayed nerves. Sometimes, the only thing she could do was listen. One sailor sobbed openly as he told her how his best friend had died in front of him; another seemed in shock over his brother's death.

As more and more men arrived, Ramsey learned of the horrors experienced by the sailors trapped inside the capsized *Oklahoma*. She heard stories of burning water, of explosions that would not stop. The shock and surprise on the men's faces were in some ways the most terrifying part of that morning.

No one had seen this coming; who could tell when it might end?

—◇—

More than any other branch of the American military, the US Navy prided itself on order and protocol. Everyone had a place, and each person had a role to play on land and sea.

But thirty minutes into the Japanese attack, it had become clear that the Navy had no plan for responding to such a brazen assault on American soil. Instead, by eight thirty that morning, ordinary sailors, soldiers, nurses, and civilians put an unofficial rescue operation into action.

Sailors dragged their wounded buddies onto land. Men with no medical training applied makeshift bandages and compresses, doing anything they could to keep the wounded alive long enough to receive proper care.

Before long, a stream of wounded men picked up speed, flowing toward Hickam Hospital. And there, the nursing staff, only six women in total, suddenly

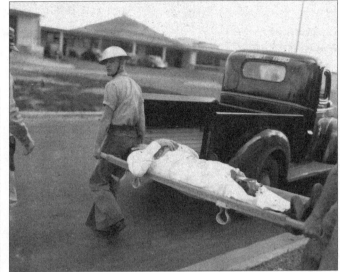

Rescuers carry a wounded Pearl Harbor
victim on a stretcher, on December 7, 1941.

found themselves on the front lines of a new, unexpected war.

A five-hundred-pound bomb exploded on the lawn outside, leaving an enormous, smoking crater. The blast caused no injuries, but the force of the shock wave caused the clocks in Hickam to stop working—a silent record of the precise moment of the Japanese attack.

Monica Conter was a highly trained Army nurse, but like all medical professionals in the US military, she had been trained to do her work many miles from the battlefront in clean, orderly hospitals. The Japanese attack on Pearl Harbor had turned all that training upside down.

The wounded staggered onto the white covered porch of Hickam Hospital on foot. Some arrived on boards or even doors—anything the able-bodied could use to get the injured to safety. Two men dragged their friend across the parking lot, his hip shattered by bullets; he arrived with a hole in his side large enough to put a fist through.

Hickam was a brand-new modern hospital with room for only thirty patients. Until the morning of December 7, the staff had treated sprained ankles, occasional broken bones, and minor illnesses. But within ten minutes of the first attack, a handful of nurses and doctors were treating hundreds of victims.

Nurses lined up stretchers holding the wounded and dying anywhere they could find space. Conter helped develop a system: Wounded men who were stable were lined up in rows on the porch, the more seriously injured were brought inside so that the small medical staff could triage their wounds, and dead men were taken around back.

So many dead men were carried in that the nurses had to stack them on the back porch, out of sight.

Some men arrived with limbs missing; others had been crushed by falling debris when a bomb landed on the nearby Army barracks; still others had been ripped apart by bomb fragments and pieces of wooden deck that had perforated their bodies. Many men arrived with gaping wounds, injuries the nurses had only read about in school. Now they rushed from patient to patient, doing anything they could to stop the bleeding.

Conter sometimes had trouble locating a spot to insert a hypodermic needle on her patients' bodies, because they had been torn to shreds from head to toe. She wiped the skin clean as best she could and then injected morphine to ease the pain. Other than a handful of alcohol sponges, she had nothing to sterilize her equipment and resorted to using the same needle on one patient after another.

When acrid smoke from the bomb blasts started to seep through the operating room windows, Conter and the other nurses rushed to plug the gaps with wet towels.

An Army pilot was dumbstruck at the sight of Conter at work. Without realizing it, she was standing in a pool of blood that had reached over the soles of her shoes.

"We were just in a daze, doing things almost automatically," Conter recalled.

The first waves of injured men suffered from shrapnel and bullet wounds from the initial bombing and strafing attacks. And then the burn victims from the *Arizona* began to arrive.

None of the staff at Hickam had ever treated so many burn injuries at one time. They knew they had to act quickly to prevent these men from going into shock, from both the extreme pain and the damage to their skin.

On the spot, Conter and her colleagues improvised a method to help stabilize these patients. The staff found a supply of "flit-guns," normally used to spray insecticide outdoors over large areas, in a supply closet. They filled these devices with tannic acid, a medicine used to treat and disinfect burns, and sprayed it all over the victims' bodies.

———◇———

With each injury they treated, the Hickam nurses dammed the flow of victims, bringing order to a chaotic morning. They took control of hundreds of patients, making snap decisions about who needed the most immediate care. They commandeered vehicles and drivers to move patients away from the battle to Tripler Hospital in Honolulu and other clinics farther away.

With little time to think, each of the nurses found her own way to fight back. "Fear didn't touch me," Mildred Clark said. "My thoughts were that I wanted to do everything I could to save every life that was there."

CHAPTER 12

BY 8:40 AM, ONCE THE LAST OF THE JAPANESE PLANES disappeared over the mountains, an eerie quiet settled over Pearl Harbor.

Small boats, braving fire and secondary explosions, bobbed on the burning water, struggling to pluck out survivors. All of Pearl Harbor seemed to darken under a sky of oily black smoke, burning lungs and stinging eyes.

Could this be the end?

After nearly twenty minutes of quiet skies, Mitsuo Fuchida's squadrons roared back in with the answer.

This time, the Japanese seemed even more determined than before, diving headlong toward the remaining battleships, destroyers, and other ships, inflicting as much damage as possible.

ATTACKED!

On the battleship *West Virginia*, an explosion sent white-hot shrapnel through the bridge, leaving Captain Mervyn Bennion slumped against a wall and bleeding heavily from his stomach. As other officers struggled to carry their dying captain to safety, a Japanese dive-bomber scored a direct hit on a large seaplane lashed to the *West Virginia*. Within seconds, fuel from the seaplane spread across the entire deck and ignited, sending flames and thick black smoke into the sky.

Dorrie Miller was working in the mess hall, deep in the bowels of the ship, when the bombs struck. The call to battle stations sent him scrambling up stairs and ladders. When he reached the outside, the noise of battle was deafening.

A commander ordered the powerfully built Miller to help him move Captain Bennion down from the bridge, which was exposed to the raging fire.

Miller and a small crew of men pulled Captain Bennion to a more sheltered spot. It proved too dangerous to lower him down steep ladders to the flaming decks below, so all they could do was try to shield him from the heat.

Miller heard the distinctive whine of an aircraft engine bearing down on the *West Virginia*. Along with one of the officers in the group, he made a dash toward an unmanned pair of .50-caliber machine guns mounted nearby. The officer watched, astonished, as Dorrie Miller readied the weapon himself and began firing at the Japanese planes attacking the ship, causing them to veer away from Captain Bennion.

Miller fired for fifteen minutes, taking charge of the desperate situation as the attackers dived again and

PHOTOGRAPHER UNKNOWN. OFFICIAL US NAVY PHOTOGRAPH, US NATIONAL ARCHIVES AND RECORDS ADMINISTRATION PHOTOGRAPHY COLLECTION.

Dorrie Miller, in a photograph taken after the Pearl Harbor attack, when he was awarded the Navy Cross for heroism.

again at the ship. In the chaos of those early moments, training, orders, and rank seemed to matter little.

Miller was not alone. Almost an hour had passed since the first bombs had fallen on Pearl Harbor. Once the initial shock had faded, thousands of men unloaded boxes of ammunition and were training their sights on the skies above. At nearby Hickam Field, from the burning decks of ships in Battleship Row, and from small craft dodging the attacking planes, more and more men mustered the presence of mind to fire back at the Japanese fighters.

The fight for Pearl Harbor was on.

The second wave of Japanese pilots noticed the change almost immediately. Pilot Zenji Abe had never flown through so much antiaircraft fire, even during his tours of duty in the war against China. Over Pearl Harbor, he was forced to pilot his dive-bomber through hundreds of exploding projectiles, whose black smoke blocked his view of the ships below.

———◆———

The night before, on his own initiative, the young watch officer Joe Taussig had ordered the second of the battleship *Nevada*'s two boilers lit, preparing for a smooth changeover of steam power from one to the other, at eight that very morning. It was good seamanship, but also a fateful move: A battleship of that size was powered by massive engines, and the ship's boilers had to be fueled and lit many hours before its twenty-foot propellers could propel the ship forward.

When the Japanese attack reached Battleship Row, every other ship in Pearl Harbor was a sitting duck. But the *Nevada*'s engines were fired up and ready to sail.

After sounding the ship's general alarm, Taussig scrambled up sets of ladders to the battleship's director, a small station that contained equipment for tracking incoming planes and pointing antiaircraft batteries in the right direction. His voice boomed over the ship.

A single Japanese torpedo plane beelined for the *Nevada*, dropping its thunderfish in the shallow waters. Seconds later, the underwater missile detonated on the ship's hull, opening up a gaping hole. The torpedo plane banked away—but exploded in the air, downed by Taussig's gunners.

Two other officers, Lieutenant Commander Francis Thomas and Chief Quartermaster Robert Sedberry, assumed command of the *Nevada*, while Taussig took charge of defending the ship from the attacking planes.

The three men decided that they had to get the ship moving: Perhaps they could even make it out of the harbor, away from the burning waters and the relentless dive-bombers.

———◇———

Charles Sehe was belowdecks as the *Nevada*'s engines churned to life and the ship pushed away from its mooring. He was in the bathroom when the torpedo struck, reading the Little Orphan Annie comic in the *Honolulu Star-Bulletin*. "The ship shuddered," Sehe recalled—but it stayed afloat.

Sehe pulled himself together and climbed up the ship's ladders to his battle station. He emerged on the open deck just as the *Nevada* passed the remains of the *Arizona*. The *Arizona*'s surface fires spread to his own ship, and Sehe could feel the intense heat.

At that moment, Sehe knew that a simple twist of fate had saved his life.

After basic training, a year earlier, Sehe's company formed a line outside a building at the Great Lakes Naval Training Station, on the banks of Lake Michigan. Each man was handed a mattress cover. At a long table inside, the men laid out their mattress covers, and an officer would mark each with the name of a ship in black ink—indicating which ship he would be assigned to. The man ahead of Sehe was the last to receive the *Arizona*'s stamp; Sehe was assigned to the *Nevada*.

"I missed being assigned to the *Arizona* by one mattress cover," Sehe said. He would almost certainly have died when the *Arizona* blew up.

Sailors on the deck of the *Nevada* tried to cover ammunition piled on the decks with their bodies, to keep it from catching fire and exploding. Fires soon spread all over the ship. Sehe and his shipmates struggled to put them out.

Listing to one side, its decks aflame, the USS *Nevada* churned toward the harbor opening, making a break for the open sea. An antiaircraft gunner on the *Nevada* named Robert Thomas looked back at the destruction. "The *West Virginia* was awash and burning, the *Oklahoma* had capsized, the *California* was listing and afire, and the *Pennsylvania*, in dry dock, was burning," he recalled. "I thought, we are the only ones left!"

Sehe, Thomas, and their crewmates could not have known the effect of their actions on the thousands of American men and women who witnessed the badly damaged *Nevada*'s escape. Cheers rang out across the water. The battleship seemed to signal that something had changed—that the Japanese attack might not succeed after all.

———◇———

Separated from the burning, smoking ships on Battleship Row, the *Nevada* made a tempting target. A wave of Japanese bombers shrieked down at the lumbering battleship.

In quick succession, five bombs found their targets, four of them crashing through the wooden decks and causing havoc in the crowded compartments below. The fifth struck just below where Joe Taussig stood as he directed antiaircraft fire against the attackers.

"I felt a tremendous blow on my leg and looked down," Taussig said, "and my left foot was under my armpit. My reaction was, 'that's a hell of a place for a foot to be.'" A red-hot piece of shrapnel had struck Taussig's thigh, completely mangling his leg.

Taussig insisted on directing the ship's antiaircraft batteries, despite his severe injury. It wasn't until several medics came and tied him to a stretcher that he finally gave up his post.

Meanwhile, because the ship was taking on more

and more water, the two other commanders decided to steer directly toward land. The huge ship beached near Hospital Point, moving with such force that the hull pushed all the way into a sugarcane field.

For Taussig, the maneuver was likely lifesaving. The men lowered him on ropes down to the main deck and then onto a launch, which ferried him to a taxi waiting at Hospital Point. He made it to Tripler General Hospital in the nick of time, where his last memory was of fading to sleep before going into the surgery that would remove what was left of his leg.

The active-duty career of one of the Navy's most promising young officers had lasted just over an hour.

———◇———

In the hectic final moments of the *Nevada*'s run, the sounds of plane engines began to fade at last. All over the harbor, men and women looked up at the sky, waiting, watching.

The Japanese did not return.

Shortly after nine thirty, the attack on Pearl Harbor was over.

In all, the Japanese strike force damaged or completely demolished twenty American ships, including eight battleships and other vessels. Almost two hundred planes were destroyed while still on the ground. Just over 2,400 American servicemen and women died in the attacks, while many hundreds more were seriously wounded.

A sailor named William Leckemby surveyed the aftermath of Japan's devastating surprise attack on the United States. "Wounded men," he said, "men without ships, men without clothing or shoes, clouds of black smoke rising in the sky, burning planes, burning ships, and confusion reigned."

———◆———

In the chaos of that morning, however, few survivors could yet comprehend all of the ways the attack had missed its mark.

By a stroke of good timing, three of the Navy's powerful aircraft carriers were out at sea when Fuchida's attackers struck Pearl Harbor—and were now prowling the surrounding waters. Other ships—including destroyers, cruisers, repair vessels, and floating hospitals—avoided damage altogether, either by sheer luck or because they were docked far away from Battleship Row. And hundreds of thousands of gallons of fuel, painstakingly transferred from the mainland to Oahu, remained unscathed in nearby storage tanks, ready to power America's inevitable counterattack.

On the morning of December 7, America's most precious resource, its people, had experienced suffering and death to an almost unimaginable degree. But those who survived, in Pearl Harbor and all across the United States, were now awake to the threat of war—and willing to join the fight.

CHAPTER 13

SEVERAL THOUSAND FEET BELOW THE PILOT ZENJI ABE, the lush green landscape of Oahu receded in the distance.

During his final pass over Pearl Harbor, a fireworks show of antiaircraft shells shook his dive-bomber when they detonated, and tracer bullets sliced through the sky, coming perilously close to his glass cockpit. In the end, he could barely see through the smoke, and as he set his compass for the rendezvous point twenty miles off the coast of Oahu, he was flying alone. Would he be able to find his fellow pilots?

Others eventually joined him over the Pacific Ocean—but not all. How many had crashed or flown off course? Most of the returning aircraft showed signs of damage, pockmarked with bullet holes or shredded by larger weapons. Together, they made their way back to the Japanese battle fleet, which was still cruising two hundred miles to the east—undetected, he hoped.

Mitsuo Fuchida stayed behind, circling over Pearl Harbor and other targets on Oahu until the very last moment, hoping to take stock of the mission's results. His attack bomber carried enough fuel for five hours' flying, and he had already been in the air for four and a half hours. Clouds of black smoke from burning diesel fuel were evidence of the Japanese squadrons' success—but they also blocked Fuchida's line of sight, and he struggled to make out the scene of destruction on the ground.

As flight commander, Fuchida also felt a personal responsibility to pick up other Japanese fighters who had strayed from the main group and lead them to safety.

The crews on the *Akagi* and other ships in the hidden strike force buzzed in anticipation of the returning aircraft. Finally, just after nine AM, the fighters and bombers from the first wave appeared through the clouds. For more than an hour, planes circled the big ships until it was their turn to land. They put down safely, one by one, on the waiting aircraft carriers.

With each safe arrival, a cheer went up from the ships.

From the flight decks, Minoru Genda and other commanders took careful note of who had returned and who had not. By ten, twenty-nine aircraft were unaccounted for and presumed destroyed. Some landed intact on the decks only to have their pilots discover that tail gunners or navigators or wingmen had not survived the Americans' intense antiaircraft barrage. And as Zenji Abe had seen firsthand, nearly all the aircraft in the Japanese force had returned home battered or damaged.

Fuchida's first priority was reporting all he had seen to Admiral Nagumo, the fleet commander, and to receive his next orders. After landing, he reported to the admiral and to his flight supervisor, Minoru Genda.

Four battleships, the pride of the US Pacific Fleet, had been completely destroyed, he told the men. Fuchida's squadrons had damaged many others, perhaps beyond repair. The Japanese pilots could not comprehend why the Americans had parked so many aircraft in the open. Their initial reports suggested that most of the United States' airpower at Pearl Harbor had gone up in smoke or was still burning on the ground.

Admiral Nagumo then turned to Fuchida and posed a question, the answer to which might well determine the future of the Japanese Empire.

"Do you think that the U.S. fleet will be able to operate out of Pearl Harbor within six months?" he asked.

Their mission was to disable the Americans long enough for Japanese forces to push south toward Indonesia, seize the rich oilfields there, and take control of so much of the Pacific and Asia that—with a weakened Navy—the United States would be forced to negotiate a diplomatic settlement.

No, Fuchida said. The Pacific Fleet was in no shape to fight again for the next six months. But then he hesitated: Perhaps it would be better to strike one more time at Pearl Harbor, to destroy more aircraft and bomb the Americans' oil supply there, which remained untouched?

Genda agreed, arguing that now was the time to crush what remained of the US forces in the Pacific.

But from the bridge of the *Akagi*, Nagumo could see what the Americans were capable of. More reports streamed in of the stiff resistance put up by antiaircraft batteries. The element of surprise was gone now. And what of the three US aircraft carriers the Japanese knew were out to sea, perhaps getting closer and closer to the hidden Japanese fleet? A single American fighter or bomber could easily stumble on the armada and alert their leaders.

"Let the enemy come!" Genda insisted. "If he does, we will shoot his planes down."

But Admiral Nagumo was in no mood to put his forces at risk. The Americans were awake now. Their gunners were reloading, their remaining fighters no doubt in the air.

In a firm voice, he ordered the Japanese fleet to set sail—for home.

———◇———

The president of the United States spent nearly all of the afternoon and evening of December 7 at his desk, taking one phone call after another and peppering his aides with questions about what, exactly, was happening at Pearl Harbor.

No direct phone line connected the American base with the White House, so news and messages had to be relayed by phone, mostly from the Navy Department in downtown Washington. So many calls came in that the president's secretary, Grace Tully, had to set up a desk outside the Oval Office with a second phone line.

It was one PM Eastern Standard Time when the first wave of Japanese attackers reached Oahu. By three, Roosevelt still had only a fragmented picture of the damage wrought by the Japanese. But it was clear that the attack on Pearl Harbor was massive, well planned, and a complete surprise. What's more, no one could assure him that the base's hundreds of advanced aircraft had managed to get into the air in time to save themselves. Each piece of news that flowed in suggested that they had not.

He worried, too, about the Imperial Japanese Navy's intentions. Was Pearl Harbor the first stop on the attackers' path to the West Coast of the United States? Was all of America now at risk?

Through the afternoon of December 7, the president and his staff struggled to distinguish fact from rumor as the nation's newspapers and wire services began to broadcast news of the attack. A crowd formed outside the White House gates, singing patriotic songs and saying prayers.

One thing Roosevelt knew for certain was that the currents of history had shifted: America was being pulled powerfully, inevitably, toward war with the Axis. Japan had struck the first blow. It was now the United States' move. And it was the president's job to explain all of this to the American people—to persuade them, without reservation, that now was the time to join the fight.

Around five, the president retired to his private study and began to compose a speech to Congress, which would also be broadcast by radio to millions of American households. Grace Tully transcribed his words as he dictated them out loud.

> *Yesterday comma December 7 comma 1941*
> *dash a date which will live in world history*
> *dash the United States of America was*
> *simultaneously and deliberately attacked by*
> *naval and air forces of the Empire of Japan.*

Tully typed it onto paper, and Roosevelt edited the words on the page with his pencil.

"Yesterday," he corrected, "December 7, 1941— *a date which will live in infamy*—the United States of America was suddenly and deliberately attacked by naval and air forces of the Empire of Japan."

He molded the text carefully to fit the gravity of the moment, knowing that all Americans would be looking to him to guide the nation through this perilous time. That evening, as he toiled alone, words were the president's most powerful weapons.

DRAFT No. 1   December 7, 1941.

PROPOSED MESSAGE TO THE CONGRESS

Yesterday, December 7, 1941, a date which will live in world history *infamy*

the United States of America was *suddenly* and deliberately attacked

by naval and air forces of the Empire of Japan.

Original typescript, with President Roosevelt's
handwritten corrections, of his speech
to Congress on December 8, 1941.

CHAPTER 14

As THE SUN BEGAN TO SET OVER OAHU, RUMORS RAN rampant. The Japanese attack had been so unexpected, and so devastating, that anything seemed possible. Did local collaborators help plan the surprise attack? Was the Imperial Japanese Navy planning a full-scale invasion of Hawaii?

Fear, suspicion, and hatred of the Japanese spread like shadows.

Soldiers and police patrolled with bayonets fixed to their rifles, questioning men and women of Asian descent on street corners, at roadblocks, and in their homes.

Guard units took up positions, fingering machine gun triggers and training their sights on anything that seemed suspicious. Jittery soldiers fired at shadows. As dusk descended, gunshots and other explosions echoed across the island—lending credence to the idea that the Japanese attackers had not yet finished the job.

In Alewa Heights, Arthur Uchida's day (which had begun with pretend war games) ended with real soldiers marching up his driveway—twelve marines, all carrying rifles. His terrified mother ran inside the house to wake Arthur's father, who had returned home earlier that afternoon after a chaotic day of helping pull sailors from burning ships.

Arthur's father demanded to know what was going on. He still had blood on his shirt from the morning's rescue operation and was wearing a Civil Defense armband.

One of the Uchidas' neighbors, the marines explained, had warned them that Arthur's family was signaling to the Japanese planes with a white flag. The marines had come to arrest the Uchida family as enemy collaborators—even though they were respected members of the community and American-born citizens.

"Oh my God, that's my flag, my white handkerchief," Arthur realized. He had put the flag there himself, that same morning, while playing with his neighborhood friends.

"I was hiding behind my father, scared to death," Arthur recalled. "I thought they were going to grab me and take me away."

Arthur's father stood his ground. "If you guys don't trust us," he said, "come in the house and search inside if you want," he said to the men. Finally, the soldiers took him at his word, and—persuaded that this was a false alarm—left the Uchidas alone.

It was a close call, but it would have been worse if the soldiers had searched Arthur's home and come to the wrong conclusions. A portrait of the emperor of Japan hung on the wall, displayed alongside a Japanese flag and a samurai sword.

"A lot of Japanese homes were like that in those days," Arthur explained. "It was sort of a symbol to recognize their parents' homeland." For as long as they could remember, the Uchidas and other Japanese Americans managed to hold on to the family's roots while also feeling at home as Americans. It was about their identity, not a sign of disloyalty. The soldiers, he was sure, would never have understood the difference and would have dragged the family away.

Hundreds of thousands of Japanese Americans would not be as lucky as the Uchidas.

An armed guard patrolling on Oahu after
the Pearl Harbor attack.

At that very moment, local Japanese people in Oahu were being rounded up for no reason other than their ancestry.

Even longtime workers at Pearl Harbor itself fell under a sudden cloud of suspicion.

Yoshiji Aoki had the day off on December 7. Born and raised in Hawaii, Aoki had become a steelworker as soon as he was old enough to work and spent his days working on battleships and other construction sites at the big Navy base. His older brother served in the military and was standing guard that day on an Oahu beach.

The next morning, December 8, Aoki returned to work for his regular seven o'clock shift at Pearl Harbor, ready to take part in the massive cleanup and rescue operations.

Without warning, a group of marines appeared and rounded up all of the Japanese American workers, assembled them in a line, and marched them out the front gate.

"About a half-mile from the gate," Aoki recalled, "I stepped out of line."

"This marine came up to me, he pointed the rifle right at me, and he told me if I stepped out of line again, he would shoot me."

"I think he meant it," Aoki said.

David Kobata, a twenty-one-year-old American citizen who drove a truck at Pearl Harbor, had a similar experience. The military authorities immediately revoked his driver's license, calling him a security risk even though he had been born in the United States. Kobata's crime: As a child, he had spent time with his grandmother, a devout Buddhist, in Hiroshima, Japan.

Shortly after the attack, Kobata was hauled into an Army barracks and interrogated about his loyalties.

"You, David Kobata, say you pledge your loyalty to the United States," the interrogator said. "Can you prove it to me by stepping on the Emperor's picture?"

The man then laid a framed portrait of the emperor of Japan on the floor.

Kobata—a proud American—explained to the man that merely stepping on a photograph did not prove or disprove loyalty to the United States.

"They let me go," Kobata said, "but when I came out of the office I had cold sweat, because I thought that if this was in Japan and I had said that, I think I would be dead by now. But, I said to myself, this is America. They respect the freedom of speech."

———◇———

The Japanese in Hawaii had followed the path of so many other immigrant groups, working hard (mostly for low wages), pushing their children ahead, and trying to preserve their culture while also becoming American. By the morning of December 8, they learned that this was not enough to be treated as equal citizens.

As she prepared breakfast, Kimiko Watanabe still had no news from her husband, Kiho, who had sailed out on his fishing boat on December 4. Her parents had gathered in her small home after the attacks—like many Japanese Americans, seeking comfort and safety among family and friends.

Kimiko was cooking a pot of rice while her son crawled on the floor when a man knocked on the door and called out to her in Japanese.

"*Oh, Kimi-chan, Kiho shinde kara, no,* Queen's Hospital *ni tsurete kitoruke,*" he said. "Oh, Kimi, Kiho has died and been brought to Queen's Hospital."

Kimiko burst into tears and dropped the pot of rice on the floor. Scooping up her infant son, she rushed with her family to the hospital, in downtown Honolulu. It was a crowded, chaotic scene as other family members milled outside and a row of soldiers prevented them from entering. No one would tell Kimiko or her family anything.

With the help of her white employer, Kimiko's sister-in-law managed to gain entrance to the local morgue, where she saw dead fishermen lined in rows, wrapped in sheets. Kiho's body lay there, too.

Kimiko was not permitted to see her husband's remains until the funeral.

Later, the story leaked out. Early in the morning on December 8, a squadron of American P-40 fighters had spotted a group of four fishing boats, including Kiho's, off the coast of Oahu. The boats had been a familiar sight in and around Honolulu for many years. But in the hours after the Japanese attack on Pearl Harbor, lines were hardening between suspected enemies (anyone who looked Japanese) and loyal Americans (anyone in the white minority).

Were the fishing boats a new wave of Japanese attackers, disguised as fishermen? The pilots did not pause to find out.

One of the surviving fishing crew recalled "water splashing around the boat...like raindrops" as the planes swooped down on the fishing fleet—only to realize seconds later that these were .50-caliber bullets, which tore through the wooden boats.

Not much remained of the tiny fleet after the initial pass by the American fighters. Six men had been killed immediately, and many more were wounded. Later an American ship rounded up the survivors, along with the dead, and transported them to Queen's Hospital in Honolulu—where they were crowded into a single room guarded by rifle-toting soldiers. The men were told that they could not speak Japanese.

Their story seeped out to the wider Japanese American community in bits and pieces, and family members learned over days and weeks about what had happened to the crews.

"Nobody came," Kimiko said. "Police or anything. To let us know anything."

Kimiko's own brother, an American soldier, did not hear about Kiho's death until the following weekend, when he visited her at home. He was shocked at the news. They were Americans. Why was their own country treating them like enemies?

CHAPTER 15

WITH THE SKIES CLEAR OF JAPANESE PLANES, IT WAS now a race against time to find anyone who might still be alive in overturned ships, demolished aircraft hangars, or the burning hulks of vessels hammered by Japanese bombs and torpedoes.

The enormous upside-down hull of the *Oklahoma* rested like a beached whale, rising thirty feet from the harbor surface at its highest point. Inside the overturned battleship, several hundred survivors stood on what used to be ceilings or treaded water in flooded compartments.

A seemingly impenetrable barrier of thick steel plates separated the men from the outside world. The only way out now was down, into the murky water, through darkened passages strewn with equipment and dead bodies, out an open porthole, and back up to the harbor surface. It would take a strong swimmer with lungs powerful enough to hold in air for several minutes—and even then, the chances of survival were slim.

A sailor named Davenport tried, twice, pulling himself down the ladder through twenty feet of water. But both times he hesitated in the pitch black, not knowing if he would make it to the surface alive.

"And then he was with us again," Stephen Bower Young recalled, "wet and stinking from the oily water, gulping for air."

More men tried and returned. And in the darkness, some of them began to notice the water slowly creeping into the chamber.

They had to get out of there.

Young could not have known it, but a group of rescuers was frantically combing the other side of the *Oklahoma*'s massive, overturned hull—searching for places to free anyone trapped inside.

When the *Oklahoma* rolled over, a native of Honolulu named Julio DeCastro rallied a group of his fellow workers from Yard Shop 11; together, they leaped into the water and swam toward the overturned hull, braving fires and the acrid smoke that wafted across the harbor from still-burning vessels.

For the next twenty-four hours, DeCastro and the other rescuers toiled methodically down the length of the exposed hull, listening for sounds of life beneath the quarter-inch steel plates.

"We could hear people pounding on the ship," one of DeCastro's crew said, "but it was deceiving because sound travels through metal. It's kind of like putting your ear to a railroad track and you can hear a train coming twenty miles away."

Men were in there, alive. But for how long?

———◆———

For seaman Charles Sehe, the most harrowing part of the *Nevada*'s journey was still to come. Enlisted men like Sehe were ordered back belowdecks, with fires still burning, to try to locate survivors—and to bring out the dead.

Steel railings, stairs, and bulkheads conducted heat from the raging oil fires; anything metal on the *Nevada* seared the skin. Moving carefully through the lower decks, Sehe got to work putting out fires so that the wounded could be evacuated safely.

That was the easy part, he discovered.

His next assignment was to recover the bodies of men killed in the blasts, many of whom Sehe had known personally as friends and shipmates. "They gave us clean, new, specially marked buckets," he said, "to go back into the casements to pick up any fragmented body parts."

He did not have to go far to find them. The casements (ship compartments) had been burned black by bomb explosions, and the force of the detonations had turned the ship's thousands of metal rivets into projectiles that shredded anything in their path. "I recall finding torn arms, legs, heads, and body torsos, and broken bones," he said, "all unidentifiable because of their blackened, flash-burned condition."

———◇———

In the bunker under Admiral Bellinger's house, Mary Ann Ramsey had spent hours caring for the wounded.

At one point, Ramsey found herself face-to-face with her terrified mother.

"I realized her face had become an ashen mask," Mary Ann recalled. Ramsey had lost herself in caring for the survivors of the attack and discovered that, unlike her mother, she still had no fear at all. Her only concern at that moment was that she wanted to do something that made a difference. "When I saw that first sailor, so horribly burned, personal fear left me," she said. "He brought to me the full tragedy of that day, drastically changing my outlook."

Pearl Harbor had transformed her.

That afternoon, the bunker occupants were finally allowed above ground. Rather than going home, Mary Ann followed the wounded to the headquarters building and spent the rest of the evening and night applying bandages, bringing drinks and food, and sitting quietly with the injured men. "I wanted to act, to do something useful, something that mattered," she said.

At the end of the evening, to her immense relief, Mary Ann's dad finally reunited with his family. She had been suppressing a terrifying thought that he might have been injured, or worse. But he was unharmed.

Captain Ramsey pulled his daughter aside and spoke to her gravely.

"The world's going to change quickly," he warned her.

But for Mary Ann Ramsey, who had grown up in a single day, her world already had.

Rescuers climb over the upturned hull of the capsized USS *Oklahoma* on December 7, 1941, hoping to locate survivors. The battleship USS *Maryland*, heavily damaged in the attack, is to the right.

———◇———

Stephen Bower Young's heart was pounding. An entire night had passed in the *Oklahoma* in silence, and now a distant rhythmic echo filled the chamber. More silence followed. Had he imagined it? His body tensed as he waited and listened.

Suddenly, the sound came back, louder and louder,

a hammer banging rapid-fire on steel. The trapped men could just about feel the vibrations traveling through the ship.

Muffled voices murmured on the other side, coming closer and closer. No more than a quarter inch of steel separated the eleven men in the compartment from the outside world. One of the men crouching near Young started pounding on the bulkhead with a hammer, signaling their location in Morse code: S-O-S, S-O-S.

On the outside, DeCastro knew he had found the spot. He hollered against the steel.

"Can you stand a hole through the bulkhead? We'll drill a small one through."

"It's okay," Young shouted back. "Go ahead!"

The whole chamber reverberated with the grinding of the drill on steel as DeCastro leaned hard into the work. Finally, he punched through, leaving a tiny hole just inches from Young's face. It was the closest any of the men had been to the outside world since the previous morning.

And then, something unexpected happened—the hammering sounds were replaced by a loud hissing noise. A long pause followed as the realization sank in: The drill hole was releasing the air pressure in the compartment. As the hissing air escaped from the small hole, the air pressure inside the chamber went down. And that pressure was the only thing holding the waters below from filling the chamber.

The men inside grew frantic. Young looked over at the compartment's bulkhead door and saw water seeping in, faster and faster.

Everything depended on a twenty-one-year-old ship-yard worker named Joe Bulgo. Working alongside DeCastro, Bulgo leaned his strong back into a hydraulic tool known as a chipping hammer, cutting a slash through the hardened steel. It was slow, exhausting work. Bulgo struggled to chisel a rectangular cut just large enough to pull a man through; but each side took him twenty minutes, and time was running out.

Inside, "it seemed like forever," one man recalled. "They had three ends cut, and finally they took a sledge-hammer and were beating that end towards us."

The water in the hold had reached their chests, and all eleven men pressed close to the inside surface of the hull.

"Look out for your hands, boys," Bulgo cried out.

The sledgehammer sang as it struck the metal.

"Again."

"And again."

At last, the steel bent forward just enough for a man to fit through.

"Okay!" Bulgo shouted. "Come on out of there! One at a time. Easy!"

He leaned in and helped pull them, one by one, into the daylight, water spilling out of the hole as Young finally made it through.

"I was out! Free! Alive!"

CHAPTER 16

ON THE NIGHT OF DECEMBER 23, NEAR THE JAPA-nese fleet's base in Kagoshima, Mitsuo Fuchida and his fellow flight crews stayed up late into the night, drinking sake and celebrating their victory over the Americans.

Fuchida had no idea how they would be treated on returning to Japan, or whether anyone would ever know the details of what had happened on that historic day. Because the planning for the attack on Pearl Harbor had taken place in total secret—and, indeed, the news was closely guarded in Japan until success was assured.

The next morning, exhausted after the two-week journey home, and with his head pounding from drinking too much alcohol the night before, he got his answer.

A message came that Fuchida and his copilot, Murata,

were to depart immediately by plane, to meet Admiral Isoroku Yamamoto, the highest-ranking officer in the Imperial Japanese Navy and one of Japan's most revered leaders. Fuchida was in no condition to fly the plane himself, and so he slept on a back bench while Murata took the pilot's seat.

Barely an hour later, the two pilots found themselves on the bridge of the aircraft carrier *Akagi*, surrounded by the Japanese Navy's top brass.

What was this about? Did Yamamoto view the mission as a success or was Fuchida's brilliant career about to come to a screeching halt?

They didn't have long to wait for an answer. One by one, Japan's top military commanders stepped forward, each one offering Fuchida toasts in his honor. In all his years as a naval officer, this was a celebration Fuchida could never have imagined.

Yamamoto himself presented Fuchida with a poem inscribed in his own traditional calligraphy, to honor the day that the flight commander brought honor and glory to the empire.

The thunderous radio broadcast of the attack

ATTACKED!

From the sky of Hawaii, 3,000 nautical miles
    away
December 8, 1941
The brilliant action of Commander Fuchida

———◆———

Two days later, Fuchida was invited to meet Emperor Hirohito himself, at the massive Yokosuka Naval Base on Tokyo Bay.

"Standing directly across from His Majesty," he recalled, "I unfolded the layout in front of him, and, pointing with my finger at the relevant places on the battlefield diagram, gave a blow-by-blow description of our battle achievements against the enemy ships."

The emperor was thrilled at Fuchida's vivid recollections of the event and by his dramatic photographs of the destruction on the Pearl Harbor bases. They spoke for over an hour as the emperor pressed him for details, pored over maps, and asked careful questions.

As Fuchida and Emperor Hirohito huddled in private, a much larger battle unfolded across a wider canvas. At that very moment, Japanese forces were surging south.

The Japanese streamed into Thailand and Burma. They secured Hong Kong, Guam, and Wake Island, all of them symbols of Western military power in the Pacific. Singapore, the British colony considered to be an impregnable fortress, fell to the Japanese Army not long after.

They broke through to the Dutch East Indies (Indonesia) in March, ejecting the Dutch colonial forces and seizing the precious oil fields that had been the main object of their plan in the first place.

Having already destroyed the large fleet of American B-17s at Clark Field in the Philippines, the Japanese then proceeded to launch an invasion of the island nation (and American protectorate). Thousands of American and Philippine troops, overwhelmed by the invaders, retreated to the Bataan peninsula near the capital, Manila. Cornered, outgunned, and starving, they finally surrendered in early May.

In a matter of months, the entire western Pacific, an area stretching from Australia in the south to the frosty waters of the Bering Strait in the north, had fallen under the control of Admiral Yamamoto, his immense fleet of ships, and his powerful squadrons of attack aircraft.

"Every day in Japan brought news of victory," Fuchida

recalled. "Somebody called it 'the Hundred Days of Glory.'"

———◆———

The attack on Pearl Harbor knocked the American military off-balance. President Roosevelt reacted furiously when he learned that America's precious fighter aircraft were caught on the ground, when they should have been in the air fending off the Japanese attackers. Inside the White House, and on the pages of the nation's newspapers, some people started pointing fingers even before all the survivors had been pulled from the burning wreckage in Pearl Harbor.

But in small towns and big cities across the United States, the Japanese managed to accomplish something that Roosevelt had been unable to do on his own.

At eleven AM on December 8, Roosevelt rose to the podium at the US Capitol to address a hastily organized emergency session of Congress. The platform bristled with microphones: More Americans tuned in to listen to the president than to any other broadcast in the history of radio.

Roosevelt had fine-tuned his speech until the wee

hours of the morning, but in the end, it lasted just six minutes and thirty seconds. Only two days earlier, Congress had been sharply split between those who wanted to avoid war at all costs (isolationists) and others who desperately wanted the United States to intervene in the fight against fascism. Now, as the president's voice soared over the chamber and his speech came to a rousing end, the entire crowd leaped to its feet to cheer him on.

Less than one hour later, speaking in near-total unanimity, both the House and Senate voted to declare war against the Empire of Japan.

"There can be no peace," the Republican speaker of the House announced to his colleagues, "until the enemy is made to pay in a full way for his dastardly deed. Let us show the world that we are a united nation."

On the morning of December 8, a man named Alan Lomax decided to travel around the country and record firsthand Americans' thoughts and feelings about the Pearl Harbor attacks. Lomax was a folklorist who worked for the Library of Congress. At a time when recording devices were incredibly rare—as well

President Roosevelt signs the US declaration of war against Japan on December 8, 1941.

as large and difficult to move—Lomax and his crew were able to capture a unique moment in the nation's history.

"I think the time has come when we should all get behind our country," a woman in Texas said.

A young man on the street in Washington, DC, declared, "I'm behind Mr. Roosevelt one hundred percent."

A man in Philadelphia, outraged at the news from Pearl Harbor, told Lomax, "We all are brothers. Let us remain brothers, don't care what creed are you or what color or who you are or where you come from. We all are American and let's fight for America and our brothers that is outside. Let's die American. If we have to go on the battlefield, let's die American."

Everywhere he went, Lomax found the same raw emotion, the same sense of unity, and the same determination.

———◇———

With America's declaration of war, new lines were being drawn on the global stage, and the pace of world events accelerated quickly.

Overnight, isolationism went into hiding; America Firsters and Nazi sympathizers, who had been holding rallies around the country, faded quickly into the shadows. Americans felt violated by the first attack on American soil since British troops had invaded the young nation during the War of 1812—but they also seemed determined not to become victims. Details of the attack on Pearl Harbor riveted Americans' attention, focusing a divided nation on a common enemy.

On December 11, Japan's ally Adolf Hitler declared war on the United States; America followed mere hours later with a unanimous declaration of war on Nazi Germany.

The Pearl Harbor attack had sealed America's entry into World War II.

———◆———

Around the time President Roosevelt was preparing to give his speech to Congress, Kazuo Sakamaki plunged into the waters off Oahu, praying he would make it to shore but believing that he might die.

He had left his home in Japan believing that the mission depended on his bravery and on his skills as a mini-sub captain. His tiny vessel, slipping carefully into the seas near Oahu, would sink one of the mighty American ships.

But Sakamaki's mission had been doomed from the moment his mini-sub launched toward the mouth of Pearl Harbor.

In the churning surf, with Battleship Row in the

distance, Sakamaki found that something was wrong: He could not steer his sub. No matter how hard he adjusted the controls, the little craft moved unpredictably, slamming into rocks and coral. They drifted in the ocean. His copilot began to cry, fearing that they would drown.

Powerful currents swept them to the far side of the island, until the little submarine crashed onto a coral reef several hundred feet from the beach. There was nothing Sakamaki and his copilot could do but try to rescue themselves as waves swept over the foundering sub and hurled them onto the rough coral. Sakamaki climbed through a tiny hatch onto the pitching deck. As waves crashed over him, he made a desperate jump into the cold ocean, swallowing salt water as he went under.

"Strength gradually went out of me," Sakamaki recalled. "Then I saw my aide no more. He was swallowed up by the giant waves. I lost consciousness."

Sakamaki woke up on a beach. He looked up and saw an American soldier standing over him. He had no strength to resist and allowed himself to be led to a nearby truck, which drove him into downtown Honolulu.

ATTACKED!

Sakamaki had left home three weeks earlier hoping to become a hero of the Japanese Empire. That morning, he had become something very different: the first prisoner of war captured by the United States in World War II.

CHAPTER 17

To THE UNITED STATES, WAR WITH JAPAN SEEMED LIKE a steady retreat from Japanese forces, at first. There was little America could do to stop the lightning-fast advance of the Imperial Japanese Navy into the warm waters of the South Pacific. Each day brought news of another Japanese victory.

President Roosevelt knew that Americans were hard at work getting the nation ready for the fight against fascism overseas. Factories that once produced cars, toasters, and radios now retooled their assembly lines to make tanks, rifles, and helmets. And in the giant shipyards of New York City, Seattle, and Los Angeles, thousands of men and women worked around the clock to rebuild the US Navy.

But after the shock of Pearl Harbor, FDR believed, Americans needed something more than a thirst for revenge to keep the war effort steaming full speed ahead. They needed a victory. They needed evidence that Japan could be defeated.

The task of showing this to the American people fell on the shoulders of an ace flier, engineer, and Army Air Forces pilot named Colonel James H. Doolittle.

Standing just five feet four inches tall, Doolittle was a giant in the field of aviation. Almost more than any other pilot alive, he had pushed the limits of what airplanes were capable of, breaking new long-distance and speed records with each passing year. Army Air Forces general Hap Arnold believed that Doolittle was the perfect leader for a mission that appeared, on the face of things, impossible.

In one sense, the plan couldn't be simpler.

Sixteen medium-range B-25 bombers, each carrying a crew of eight men, would take off from the USS *Hornet*, a small aircraft carrier. The *Hornet* would sail to within six hundred miles of the Japanese home islands, taking the bombers to within range of the Japanese capital. Flying without fighter escorts to protect them (because fighters could not fly that far without refueling), the B-25 crews would launch a daring, daytime bombing raid on Tokyo, flying low to the ground to avoid detection.

Doolittle believed that it could be done. But the scheme came with risks that no aircrew had ever faced during wartime.

The plan called for the sixteen large aircraft to be crammed onto the *Hornet*'s deck, leaving no room for maneuver—or error. But no bomber of that size had ever successfully taken off from an aircraft carrier.

If they could manage to take off from the *Hornet*, the risks grew even more extreme. Once in the air, the B-25s could never land safely back on the aircraft carrier deck: This was a one-way trip. Using maps, and relying on little more than their wits, the pilots were instructed to fly to China after the raid, crossing over the Sea of Japan and doing whatever they could to land in territory occupied by friendly Chinese forces.

They might put down in fields or crash-land on beaches—or even in the ocean. Some might be shot down over Japan. Nobody knew for sure.

———◇———

ATTACKED!

On April 2, 1942, Doolittle's raiders set sail from San Francisco Bay on the *Hornet*, accompanied by a small group of ships that would protect them and allow them to refuel along the way.

The small convoy had been traveling for over two weeks when, early in the morning on April 18, American lookouts spotted two large Japanese fishing vessels in the distance. There was no question a fisherman had spotted them—and the American commanders had to assume that the Japanese had radioed their discovery to the Imperial Navy.

It was now or never. Admiral William Halsey, the fleet commander, gave the order for the raid to proceed—even though they were still *four hundred* miles from their planned launch point.

The extra four hundred miles tacked onto their journey meant that the B-25s' fuel supplies would be stretched to the absolute limit. At the last minute, the *Hornet's* crew squeezed several five-gallon cans of extra fuel onto each plane. Every ounce of fuel meant a few more minutes in the air, a few extra chances to make it to safety.

"The way things are now, we have about enough to get us within 200 miles of the China coast, and that's all," one pilot said to his crew. He had checked the maps, calculated the distance, and concluded that making it to safety was all but impossible. "If anyone wants to withdraw," he told his men, "he can do it now. We can replace him from the men who are going to be left aboard. Nothing will ever be said about it, and it won't be held against you. It's your right. It's up to you."

Not a single man chose to stay behind.

"I was scared," one crew member recalled. "We knew the odds were against us."

Doolittle's bomber shook, its engines roaring, wheels straining hard against its brakes and against the cables lashing it to the *Hornet*. When the signal finally came, the B-25 lurched forward across the short flight deck, the choppy waters of the North Pacific approaching fast.

To the crews on the *Hornet*, Doolittle's B-25 seemed to disappear at first, dropping below the line where the forward deck ended. And then, a few seconds later, its dark shape reappeared on the horizon. Doolittle banked his plane to the right as it rose into the gray sky, tracing a wide circle around the fleet.

One by one, fifteen more B-25s followed him into the

air. Before this very moment, no one had truly believed that so many heavily loaded bombers could take off from an aircraft carrier without crashing into the sea. The aircrews had achieved the impossible. The raid was on.

———◇———

The crews had given their bombers plucky names, painted brightly on their fuselages: *Ruptured Duck*. *Fickle Finger of Fate*. *Bat Out of Hell*.

The squadron soared low over the ocean, to keep Japanese patrols from spotting them. Now and then, a crew would toss an empty five-gallon fuel can into the water after refilling the tank and it would skitter over the waves.

Almost certainly, Doolittle thought, the fishing boats had alerted the Japanese high command. The Imperial Navy's fearsome, nimble Zero fighters would be hunting for his squadron as the Americans made their approach, and the B-25s could only do so much to defend themselves. Everything depended on timing and luck. Doolittle understood that he might not make it—but, above all, he wanted to get to Tokyo before the Japanese got to him and his men.

Around a quarter to noon, the first of Doolittle's

raiders crossed over the shoreline and pressed on toward Tokyo. No outside invader had reached Japan in over 2,500 years.

"It was a beautiful spring day with not a cloud in the sky," one crew member wrote in his diary. "The Japanese country is beautiful and their towns look like children's play gardens. It is a shame to bomb them but they asked for it."

People on the ground waved at the planes as they cruised overhead, sometimes as low as fifty feet. One crew even saw a baseball game underway. Nobody, it seemed, understood that the Americans had come.

The mission's planners had given each of Doolittle's crews a different target to strike. A Japanese army barracks. A naval shipyard. A torpedo factory. A munitions plant. Each B-25 approached Tokyo from a different direction, hoping to scramble the Japanese defenses and sow chaos below.

As each aircraft made its final approach, the pilots pulled up on their controls, soaring up to two thousand feet in the air so that the bombardiers, peering through carefully calibrated bombsights, could home in on their objectives. A red indicator light flashed when the bomb doors opened. At the precise second, the bombardier pressed hard on a trigger, and four large bombs (or "eggs," as the crews dubbed them) tumbled toward the ground below.

"This was it, our answer for Pearl Harbor," one of the men said out loud.

———◇———

The first bombs struck just after noon. Over the next three hours, the American planes crisscrossed the Japanese capital, dropping their deadly payloads on the city below.

For the Japanese people on the receiving end, the Doolittle raiders brought home the terror and arbitrariness of air war.

One bomb detonated among a group of workers on their lunch break, instantly killing twelve of them.

Another exploded in a group of wooden homes, killing six people, including two children.

One American tail gunner opened fire at what he believed to be a military barracks with a guard tower atop it. As they flew past, the man recounted that "I saw fifteen to twenty bodies which had fallen as if they were hit by our bombardier's fire." But these were not soldiers or even adults, because it wasn't a military barracks at all: They were students at the Mizumoto Primary School who had scattered in terror and were caught out in the open as bullets rained down on them.

In all, over fifty Japanese civilians perished in the attacks. For hours after the last plane disappeared in the distance, a haze of smoke lingered over Tokyo as fires burned and sirens wailed through the city streets.

Meanwhile, not a single Doolittle raider had been shot down.

———◇———

Their mission accomplished, the Doolittle raiders now faced the most daunting part of their journey.

One after another, and spaced out across hundreds of miles, the B-25s roared over the East China Sea, leaving the Japanese mainland behind. Their gas tanks, already running low when they passed over Tokyo, now were close to empty. Foul weather moved in over the ocean, making it almost impossible to see the approaching coast of China.

Each crew was forced to make its own, sometimes desperate decision.

One B-25 veered north toward the Soviet city of Vladivostok, in a last-ditch bid to land safely, far from

Japanese forces. Other crews crash-landed in the sea, tumbling into the frigid water and swimming frantically to shore. Still others bailed out into the black night, parachuting into what they hoped would be friendly territory. One pilot pulled off a daring landing on a mud flat, wrecking the plane but leaving his entire crew unharmed.

One man parachuted into a tree. Many were seriously injured with broken bones and deep lacerations. In the darkness, men rolled themselves up in their parachutes to fend off the rain and cold. Doolittle himself hid in an abandoned mill and did exercises all night to stay warm.

The next morning, alone or in small groups, the survivors hiked down remote mountain paths, searching for other Americans or for Nationalist Chinese soldiers—America's allies in the fight against Japan. The raiders had scattered over four hundred miles of Chinese territory, some of it teeming with hostile Japanese troops.

For weeks, often with the help of search parties, survivors trickled in to the regional capital of Chongqing, where Doolittle had set up a base. By the end of April, almost sixty men found their way to him, hungry and injured, but alive.

Colonel James Doolittle, fourth from right,
poses with several members of his raiders and
with Chinese allies, following his crash landing.

Three men died during crash landings, and Japanese forces in China captured sixteen others. Some of these sat out the war in Japanese prison camps—but the Japanese executed three others in October 1942.

Fourteen of the original flight crews eventually returned safely to the United States.

What began as a one-way mission for Doolittle's raiders became a triumphant round-trip journey home.

ATTACKED!

---❖---

Measured by the damage it caused, the Doolittle Raid was no Pearl Harbor. Japan's war machine remained untouched. Its navy still prowled the Pacific, ready to take on any attempt to thwart its ambitions.

But the eighty men who put their lives at risk, on a mission with no hope of return, broadcast a powerful message. To the Japanese leadership, the Doolittle Raid announced that the Pearl Harbor attack had not cowed the United States into submission.

And Doolittle and his crews assured the American people that Pearl Harbor was the beginning, not the end. American men and women, of all backgrounds, were joining this fight for the long haul.

Office of War Information, US Government Printing Office, 1941.

One of thousands of different posters
printed by the US government after
the Pearl Harbor attacks.

EPILOGUE

Pearl Harbor Memories

THE US GOVERNMENT MADE SURE AMERICANS WOULD remember December 7. In constant news broadcasts and on recruitment posters plastered just about everywhere, images of the attack and the words Pearl Harbor were used to remind all Americans that Japan's unjustified assault on American soil must be avenged.

Pearl Harbor became a symbol. It gave Americans on the front lines and the home front a justification for why they were fighting, and why the war had to be won. America had been caught off guard, it said, and suffered the consequences—but this would never, ever happen again.

This "official" story of Pearl Harbor cast a long shadow. Though it contained elements of truth, it also outshined many other, very different memories of Pearl Harbor and different ways of understanding that world-changing day.

———◇———

Donald Keli'inoi's family lost its land for good to the US Navy, which was hungry to expand its base at Pearl Harbor. "We lost it because of the war," Donald said. "We might have been millionaires today if we still had that land. Who knows?"

The Keli'inois, like so many other Hawaiians, never regained what they lost during the war. For them, Pearl Harbor was one chapter in a longer story of how America stole Hawaii from its native inhabitants.

For Donald Keli'inoi, the damage of the Pearl Harbor attack lasted well beyond December 7—and even beyond the end of World War II.

———◇———

Mitsuo Fuchida became a national hero in Japan for his role in the Pearl Harbor attack. After Japan's defeat in 1945, Fuchida became outraged at the war crimes trials conducted in Japan by the American occupation authorities, which were meant to punish Japan's military leaders for atrocities committed against the Chinese, prisoners of war, and others. But during that same period in his life, he came across a story that dramatically changed his outlook.

Fuchida read a pamphlet written by Jacob DeShazer, one of the Doolittle raiders who had been captured during the 1942 raid over Tokyo. DeShazer described his harsh treatment by his Japanese captors—including torture—but also his desire to forgive and his unwillingness to hate his former enemies. Following his release, DeShazer had become a Christian missionary in Japan.

Deeply moved by DeShazer's account, Mitsuo Fuchida decided to convert to Christianity himself and to become an outspoken opponent of war. He spent many years touring the United States as a Christian missionary, giving speeches and sermons to large crowds across the country. He even met with the family members of American servicemen killed in the Japanese attack on Pearl Harbor and visited Oahu on the twenty-fifth anniversary of the attack. His own children moved to the United States permanently and became American citizens.

Many Americans saw Pearl Harbor as the reason that America should always be ready for war; Mitsuo Fuchida concluded that the suffering experienced that day was an argument for fighting for peace.

—◇—

Six days after the Pearl Harbor attacks, Logan Ramsey informed Mary Ann and her mother that they had forty-five minutes to pack their suitcases. They would be returning to the mainland United States on a flight—without him. The US Navy was about to make Pearl Harbor the home base for the largest military buildup in American history, and it was no place for children.

Less than an hour later, shocked and somber, Mary Ann Ramsey boarded a Pan American Airways plane. It was, she said, "the first and probably saddest flight of my life." She had arrived in Pearl Harbor full of hope for a stable, bright future; she left under a cloud of war and uncertainty.

—◇—

Dorrie Miller's Navy career was typical of the more than one hundred thousand Black men who served in the Navy during World War II. Despite having been awarded the Navy Cross for his bravery during the Pearl Harbor attack, Miller returned to his job as a mess attendant, serving white enlisted men and officers belowdecks.

For Black people, the new war had two goals: victory overseas against fascism and victory on the home front against racial discrimination. "Double V" became their rallying cry.

After Pearl Harbor, Miller was promoted to cook third class aboard the USS *Liscome Bay*, a Navy escort ship. He was still toiling in the kitchen when the *Liscome Bay* sailed from Pearl Harbor in the fall of 1943. On November 23, a Japanese submarine sighted the American ship and destroyed it with a single torpedo. The *Liscome Bay* exploded and sank to the bottom of the Pacific Ocean. Miller drowned with more than six hundred of his fellow crew members.

In 2020, the US Navy announced that it would name its newest aircraft carrier after the mess attendant who helped repel the Japanese attack on Pearl Harbor. The USS *Doris Miller* is scheduled to enter service in October 2029.

———◇———

Kimiko Watanabe went back to work after her husband Kiho's death—first as a waitress at a local restaurant and then at a pineapple cannery. She could never bring herself to visit his gravesite at the Mo'ili'ili Japanese Cemetery on Oahu. Instead, every year, she took a bouquet of flowers to her church to honor Kiho's memory. No one in the US government ever apologized to her for killing her husband.

To the Japanese American community in Hawaii, the third attack wave hit hard—but it came from their fellow American citizens, not from the Empire of Japan.

All of a sudden, signs of Japanese identity and culture became suspect, if not outright illegal. The government shut down Japanese-language schools and clubs, calling on the Japanese American community to "speak American." Teahouses all over the islands had to lock their doors for good—and the women who depended on them for work, many of them elderly, joined the ranks of the unemployed. Kimonos and Japanese sandals, once a common sight, disappeared from view. Buddhist priests could no longer practice their faith or minister to their congregations. Telephone operators even eavesdropped on conversations, and if any party spoke Japanese, the call was disconnected.

As bad as things were for Hawaii's Japanese American community, they soon learned that the situation for Japanese Americans on the mainland was even worse.

On February 19, 1942, President Roosevelt signed Executive Order 9066, which instructed the military to round up Americans of Japanese ancestry living on the West Coast and imprison them in closely guarded internment camps. In a shocking violation of their constitutional rights, nearly 130,000 people (half of whom were children) were forcibly torn from their homes, businesses, and farms—leaving behind their livelihoods, friends, and possessions. Most spent the war years in remote desert camps, sometimes separated from their loved ones.

The military authorities on Hawaii harbored deep suspicions about the islands' Japanese American residents. Hawaii's Japanese American community was subjected to constant surveillance, harassment, and even detention without trial.

America's Japanese American citizens experienced Pearl Harbor's aftermath as a betrayal—by their own country, the United States. For them, the experience was a warning of how fragile our democracy can be and of how easily racism can determine whose rights are protected and whose are not.

———◆———

Monica Conter and the five other Hickam nurses spent the three weeks following the attack working around the clock to care for survivors; one particularly grueling shift lasted thirty hours. Finally, in late December, the Army sent two relief nurses to Hickam, making the care of the wounded more manageable.

In a letter home, Conter expressed the deep sense of purpose she and her colleagues felt about their work. "Tell everyone I couldn't have missed it for anything," she wrote to her parents. It was a feeling that stayed with her for the rest of her life—the sense that, as a caregiver, she had helped America bounce back from disaster.

Pearl Harbor was a proving ground for the Army Nurse Corps—and a live rehearsal for the four years of war that followed. The experience on December 7 and 8 showed that nurses could treat patients and save lives close to the front lines of battle. By 1945, almost sixty thousand American women served as Army nurses, and their courage and training ensured that more injured American soldiers survived in this war than in any previous conflict.

---◇---

For most Pearl Harbor survivors, the switch from peace to war happened overnight, and men like Charles Sehe found themselves preparing for the next battle even as the smoke from the Japanese attack still hung over the water.

The ingenuity of the Imperial Japanese Navy, combined with the mistakes of America's military and political leaders, made the attack on Pearl Harbor a surprise of epic proportions. But what prevented it from becoming a *defeat* was the thousands of men and women who met the challenge of that day, in the fire and heat of the attacks of December 7. Their responses to adversity, as much as the bold leadership of FDR and his cabinet, defined the new path the nation would take in the months and years that followed.

It would take decades for the United States to acknowledge not only the victims of the Japanese attack but the contributions of those men and women who survived.

Many years later, Sehe still thought about a friend who had narrowly survived the attack on the *Nevada* but had been badly burned. "He's still living in Tennessee," Sehe told an interviewer. "He's still taking pain pills. They didn't know much about burn treatment at the time."

"All those men that were lost," Sehe reflected. "Why, I don't know. I was just so damn lucky. But, why me?"

———◆———

For more than twenty years, the USS *Arizona* sat at the bottom of Pearl Harbor, with a single flagpole raised over the wreck to commemorate the 1,177 who died there on the morning of December 7, 1941—including the 900 who were never recovered.

Finally, in 1962, the National Park Service completed construction of a floating memorial platform, which sits over the remains of the *Arizona*'s massive submerged hull.

Millions of Americans visit the *Arizona* memorial each year.

ATTACKED!

————◇————

Eighty years after the USS *Oklahoma* flipped over, researchers from the US Defense Department completed the painstaking task of examining the remains of unidentified victims, using newly available DNA evidence. They were eventually able to confirm the identities of 343 sailors and marines.

In July 2021, the Navy returned the remains of Louis Tushla, who was only twenty-five when he was killed on the *Oklahoma*, to his family in Atkinson, Nebraska. He was buried in a local cemetery, with little fanfare, next to his parents.

That summer, in such quiet and private moments, families across the United States were finally able to close a door on the history of Pearl Harbor, putting to rest victims of the attacks whose names had never appeared in the history books.

But the memories of Pearl Harbor live on—and the lessons of that terrible day can be gleaned from the stories and actions of those who survived, and those who did not.

Can we ever truly be prepared for the unexpected,

or is the secret not in the preparation but in *how* we respond to what history throws at us? On a December morning in 1941, the men, women, and children who bore the brunt of the attacks found their own answers.

Many fought back bravely.

Some found new powers within themselves.

Some helped those in distress.

Some steered a course to safety.

Some refused to give in to blame or suspicion.

Some stood up for their rights, against the odds. Still others fell victim to events beyond their control—but managed to come back, over time, and build new lives.

Their answers shape our history and speak to us still, long after the living memories of Pearl Harbor have faded.

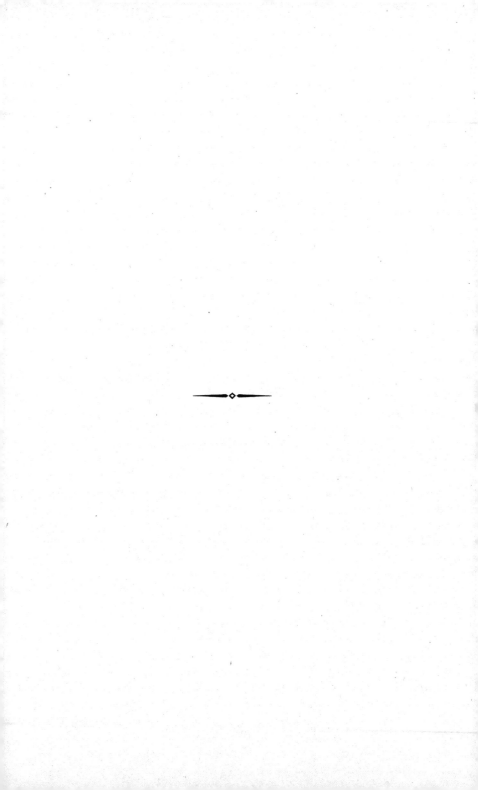

ACKNOWLEDGMENTS

THE PATH TO THIS BOOK WAS BLAZED BY THE WISE
Tanya McKinnon, whose counsel I am grateful for every
time I clear my cluttered desk and begin writing. Without the brilliant Lisa Yoskowitz at Little, Brown Books
for Young Readers, there would be no book to speak
of; Lisa's editorial acumen shaped the final product
on all levels. Lily Choi contributed an essential round
of edits that improved the manuscript materially. My
appreciation also goes out to Caitlyn Averett for her support throughout, as well as others on the LBYR team,
including Patricia Alvarado, Andy Ball, Rick Ball, Mara
Brashem, Gabrielle Chang, Andie Divelbiss, Bill Grace,
David Koral, Jen Graham, Karina Granda, Amber Mercado, Christie Michel, Victoria Stapleton, and Lara Stelmaszyk, who made vital contributions to this project.

All historical writing builds on the work and generosity of others. In this case, my specific thanks go
out to Gwyneth Rhiannon Milbrath for pointing me

ACKNOWLEDGMENTS

to essential sources on the history of Pearl Harbor nurses—and even sharing documents that would have been inaccessible to me otherwise. Chris Dixon of Macquarie University shared important context and sources for the African American experience at Pearl Harbor and in the Pacific War. Martha Elmore in the Special Collections Department at the East Carolina University Library provided access to oral history transcripts with Joseph Taussig Jr. Thanks also to Sherman Seki at the University of Hawaiʻi at Mānoa Library and Ed Lynch at the *Honolulu Star-Advertiser* for help accessing and obtaining permission for crucial photographs.

My peeps on the home front—Patty, Owen, and Emmett—give me the motive to write in the first place.

PACIFIC WAR AND WORLD WAR II TIMELINE

1931
The Imperial Japanese Army invades Manchuria.

1937
Japan declares war on China.

1940
Adolf Hitler invades the Netherlands, Belgium, Luxembourg, and France.

1941
Hitler invades the Soviet Union; Japan invades Indochina, setting off a new diplomatic crisis with the United States.

1941
President Roosevelt orders a total embargo on the sale of oil to Japan.

December 7, 1941
Japan attacks Pearl Harbor, demolishing much of the US Pacific Fleet and killing more than 2,400 Americans.

December 8, 1941
The United States declares war on Japan.

December 11, 1941
Adolf Hitler declares war on the United States; hours later, the United States declares war on Germany, sealing America's entry into World War II.

May 7, 1945
Germany surrenders to the
United States and its allies.

August 6 and 9, 1945
The United States drops atomic
bombs on the Japanese cities of
Hiroshima and Nagasaki.

**August 15, 1945
(August 14 in the
United States)**
Emperor Hirohito announces
Japan's unconditional surrender
to the United States.

1962
USS *Arizona* Memorial
opens in Pearl Harbor.

DECEMBER 7, 1941: THE ATTACK ON PEARL HARBOR TIMELINE

5:50 AM
The first wave of Japanese attackers takes off from aircraft carriers 230 miles off the coast of Oahu.

7:02 AM
The radar station at Opana reports a large incoming flight of aircraft and mistakenly identifies it as American.

7:53 AM
Flight commander Mitsuo Fuchida, at the head of the first attack wave, reaches the shores of Oahu undetected.

7:55 AM
Japanese planes make their first strikes on Ford Island and other air bases across the island. Japanese torpedo bombers launch their first torpedoes toward Battleship Row, striking the USS *Arizona* and USS *California*.

8:00 AM
The *Oklahoma* capsizes.

8:00–8:05 AM
Numerous other ships, including the USS *Arizona* and USS *Utah*, are struck by torpedoes. Japanese "horizonal bombers" launch a high-altitude bombing attack against Ford Island and Battleship Row.

8:06 AM
The USS *Arizona* is struck by bombs and explodes, killing more than 1,100 men.

8:40 AM
The first Japanese attack wave ends.

8:53 AM
The second Japanese attack wave reaches Pearl Harbor. The USS *Nevada* tries to steam away from Battleship Row but is struck repeatedly by Japanese torpedoes and bombs; the battleship is forced to beach itself on Hospital Point.

10:10 AM
The last Japanese fighters depart Pearl Harbor.

1:00 PM
The Japanese fleet returns home.

SOURCE NOTES

CHAPTER 1

4 "How many naval vessels are docked?": Takeo Yoshikawa and Andrew Mitchell, *Japan's Spy at Pearl Harbor: Memoir of an Imperial Navy Secret Agent* (Jefferson, NC: McFarland Books, 2020), 108.

8 "Lights were flickering all over": Ibid., 85.

CHAPTER 2

15 "Day in, day out, you just saw each other": Lawrence Rodriggs, *We Remember Pearl Harbor* (Newark, CA: Communications Concepts, 1991), 97.

18 "I remained unreconciled to my Hawaiian prospects": Mary Ann Ramsey, "Only Yesteryear," U.S. Naval Institute, *Naval History*, Winter 1991, 1.

18 "We were literally surrounded by them": Ibid., 2.

CHAPTER 3

20 "War with America!": Ensign Kazuo Sakamaki, *I Attacked Pearl Harbor: The True Story Told by the Midget Submarine Officer Who Became United States P.O.W. #1*, trans. Toru Matsumoto, ed. Gary R. Coover (Honolulu: Rollston Press, 2017), 15.

22 "One mistake on the part of any one of you may be fatal to all of us": Ibid., 16.

22 "Here is something we must have": Ibid., 17.

22 *I am now leaving. I owe you, my parents, a debt I shall never be able to repay*: Ibid.

23 "I was saying good-bye to all things to which a normal person clings": Ibid., 18.

26 "On December 8, we will attack and destroy the US fleet at Pearl Harbor": Juzo Mori, *The Miraculous Torpedo Squadron*, trans. Nicholas Voge (self-published, 2015), e-book location 1488.

28 "She was also making strange groaning noises, as if fighting for her life against a sea that would tear her apart": Ibid., location 1627.

CHAPTER 4

32 "No one could sink a battleship": Stephen Bower Young, *Trapped at Pearl Harbor: Escape from Battleship* Oklahoma (Annapolis, MD: Naval Institute Press, 2013), 32.

33 "I am what you call a Depression-era child": Interview with Charles Sehe, December 8, 2001, Admiral Nimitz Historic Site, Center for Pacific War Studies, Fredericksburg, VA, 1.

35 "I was getting a real education": Captain Joseph K. Taussig, Jr., November 19, 1987, Oral History Interview 91, East Carolina Manuscript Collection, 4.

36 "the only way Negroes can die in Uncle Sam's democratic Navy is slinging hash": Thomas W. Cutrer and T. Michael Parrish, *Doris Miller, Pearl Harbor, and the Birth of the Civil Rights Movement* (College Station: Texas A&M University Press, 2018), e-book location 371.

36 "it beats sitting around Waco working as a busboy, going nowhere": Ibid., e-book location 349.

37 "It was very exciting": Gwyneth Rhiannon Milbrath, MSN, RN, "We Just Had to Line Them Up," in Monica Conter, Army Nurse Corps, *Windows in Time: The Newsletter of the University of Virginia School of Nursing Eleanor Crowder Bjoring Center for Nursing Historical Inquiry* 22, no. 2 (October 2014), 9.

38 *This war situation is really something*: Ibid.

SOURCE NOTES

39 "We were just overwhelmed": Ibid., 10.

39 "My family, my village, the navy, and my country—they were depending on me": Ensign Kazuo Sakamaki, *I Attacked Pearl Harbor: The True Story Told by the Midget Submarine Officer Who Became United States P.O.W. #1*, trans. Toru Matsumoto, ed. Gary R. Coover (Honolulu: Rollston Press, 2017), 35.

CHAPTER 5

41 "I am confident that both of us have a sacred duty to restore traditional amity and prevent further death and destruction": Franklin D. Roosevelt, "Appeal to Emperor Hirohito to Avoid War in the Pacific," December 6, 1941, posted online by Gerhard Peters and John T. Woolley, American Presidency Project, https://www.presidency.ucsb.edu/node/210391.

42 "This means war": Steven M. Gillon, *Pearl Harbor: FDR Leads the Nation into War* (New York: Basic Books, 2011), 35.

44 "Be on the alert accordingly": Nigel Hamilton, *The Mantle of Command: FDR at War, 1941–42* (New York: Mariner Books, 2015), 51.

47 "Japan would now wield the sword of righteousness": Juzo Mori, *The Miraculous Torpedo Squadron*, trans. Nicholas Voge (self-published, 2015), e-book location 1653.

49 "Start your engines": Mitsuo Fuchida, *For That One Day: The Memoirs of Mitsuo Fuchida, Commander of the Attack on Pearl Harbor*, trans. Douglas T. Shinsato and Tadamori Urabe (self-published by the translators, 2001), 86.

50 "My back was wet with sweat": Mori, *The Miraculous Torpedo Squadron*, location 1720.

CHAPTER 6

55 "It was a tropical post": Mary Klaus, "Remembering: Joseph Lockard, Was in the Army During Pearl Harbor Attack," PennLive, *Patriot News*, December 7, 2012, https://www.pennlive.com/midstate/2012/12/remembering_joseph_lockard_was.html.

SOURCE NOTES

57 "It was possible to pick up one plane...and it was also sometimes *im*possible to pick up three or four": Testimony of Lieutenant Joseph Lockard, *Pearl Harbor Attack, Hearings Before the Joint Committee on the Investigation of the Pearl Harbor Attack,* Congress of the United States, Part 27, 477.

58 "I fooled around some more trying to determine exactly whether it was something coming in": *Ibid,* 531.

59 "Call the information center and see if there is anyone around": Ibid.

60 "I have never seen anything like this": Testimony of Colonel Kermit Tyler, *Pearl Harbor Attack, Hearings Before the Joint Committee on the Investigation of the Pearl Harbor Attack,* Congress of the United States, Part 27, 569.

60 "You see, I had a friend who was a bomber pilot": Ibid.

60 "Don't worry about it": Daniel Allen Butler, *Pearl: December 7, 1941* (Philadelphia: Casemate Publishers, 2020), 183.

61 "Finally, a white line appeared": Warren R. Schmidt, "Lieutenant Zenji Abe: A Japanese Pilot Remembers," HistoryNet, June 12, 2006, https://www.historynet.com/lieutenant-zenji-abe-a -japanese-pilot-remembers/.

62 "*Tora! Tora! Tora!*": Mitsuo Fuchida, *For That One Day: The Memoirs of Mitsuo Fuchida, Commander of the Attack on Pearl Harbor,* trans. Douglas T. Shinsato and Tadamori Urabe (self-published book by the translators, 2001), 86.

63 "They've changed the color of our planes!": Craig Nelson, *Pearl Harbor: From Infamy to Greatness* (New York: Scribner, 2016), 207.

CHAPTER 7

67 "The entire island seemed to be blowing up": Mary Ann Ramsey, "Only Yesteryear," U.S. Naval Institute, *Naval History,* Winter 1991, 2.

67 "What is this? Drills on a Sunday?": Stephen Bower Young, *Trapped at Pearl Harbor: Escape from Battleship Oklahoma* (Annapolis, MD: Naval Institute Press, 2013), 27.

SOURCE NOTES

68 "Blood spattered all over me": Craig Nelson, *Pearl Harbor: From Infamy to Greatness* (New York: Scribner, 2016), 266.

69 "None of us thought about bombs": Robert S. LaForte and Ronald E. Marcello, eds., *Remembering Pearl Harbor: Eyewitness Accounts by U.S. Military Men and Women* (Wilmington, DE: SR Books, 1991), 28.

71 "As we hit the ground": Roy Reid, oral history interview with Jack Sigler, April 11, 2002, 2.

72 "Who is it, Marie?": Ibid., 4.

73 "There's a message from the signal tower saying the Japanese are attacking Pearl Harbor and this is no drill": Steve Twomey, *Countdown to Pearl Harbor: The Twelve Days to the Attack* (New York: Simon & Schuster, 2016), 277.

73 "was as white as the uniform he wore": Nelson, *Pearl Harbor*, 260.

CHAPTER 8

75 "The hangars were aflame and the planes on the ground were burning": Thomas Allen, *Remember Pearl Harbor: American and Japanese Survivors Tell Their Stories* (New York: National Geographic Kids, 2016), 26.

75 "It now seemed hard to believe": Juzo Mori, *The Miraculous Torpedo Squadron*, trans. Nicholas Voge (self-published, 2015), e-book location 1798.

76 "If they had placed torpedo nets on their exposed sides": Ibid., location 1800.

76 "I felt the plane leap skywards as the heavy torpedo dropped away": Ibid., location 1842.

77 "Suddenly I spotted two wakes heading for the ship": Craig Nelson, *Pearl Harbor: From Infamy to Greatness* (New York: Scribner, 2016), 262.

81 "We're trapped": Stephen Bower Young, *Trapped at Pearl Harbor: Escape from Battleship* Oklahoma (Annapolis, MD: Naval Institute Press, 2013), 80.

82 "I surfaced, gulped for air, and automatically began to swim": Ibid., 77.

SOURCE NOTES

82 "Here, over here": Ibid., 78.

82 "We had to do something, anything, to get out of here": Ibid., 120.

CHAPTER 9

83 "You could see the wake of the torpedo and it looked like it was coming to you": Craig Nelson, *Pearl Harbor: From Infamy to Greatness* (New York: Scribner, 2016), 280.

84 "You could feel the decks—the compartments—being penetrated": Robert S. LaForte and Ronald E. Marcello, eds., *Remembering Pearl Harbor: Eyewitness Accounts by U.S. Military Men and Women* (Wilmington, DE: SR Books, 1991), 18.

85 "I was petrified": Ibid., 29.

86 "I was trying to get under cover": Ibid.

88 "I remember lots of steel and bodies coming down": Ibid., 30.

88 "The ship had become a piece of molten steel, a kind of giant tea kettle": Paul Joseph Travers, *Eyewitness to Infamy: An Oral History of Pearl Harbor, December 7, 1941* (Lanham, MD: Madison Books, 1991), 141.

89 "There were bodies of men": Ibid., 19.

90 "People who have never seen this at sea cannot imagine what oil is like once it is exposed to cool seawater": Ibid., 20.

90 "The most vivid recording in my memory bank of that ordeal": Harry Spiller, *Pearl Harbor Survivors: An Oral History of 24 Servicemen* (Jefferson, NC: McFarland & Company, Inc., 2002), 125.

CHAPTER 10

93 "Hey, we got something going on out there": Lawrence Rodriggs, *We Remember Pearl Harbor* (Newark, CA: Communications Concepts, 1991), 98.

93 "It was as if someone took a pick and dug up our front yard—the dirt was bouncing up": Ibid., 99.

94 "We were so far out in the boonies": Ibid., 100.

SOURCE NOTES

95 "As soon as we got out of the house": Ibid., 125.

97 "We actually saw planes dive-bombing": Ibid., 127.

99 "Oh Kimiko, over there *senseo natta itte kara*": Oral history interview with Kimiko Watanabe, April 21, 1992, Waialua, Oahu, "An Era of Change: Oral Histories of Civilians in World War II Hawaii," Center for Oral History, University of Hawai'i at Mano'a, 1313.

CHAPTER 11

104 "A young man, filthy black oil covering his burned, shredded flesh, walked in unaided": Mary Ann Ramsey, "Only Yesteryear," U.S. Naval Institute, *Naval History*, Winter 1991, 3.

110 "We were just in a daze, doing things almost automatically": Monica Conter Benning, interview, May 26, 1982, with Patricia Sloane, Ed.D., U.S. Army Nurse Corps Oral History Program, 21.

111 "Fear didn't touch me": Oral history interview, May 25, 1982, with Colonel Mildred Irene Clark, conducted by Patricia Sloan, Ed.D., U.S. Army Nurse Corps Oral History Program, 21.

CHAPTER 12

117 "The ship shuddered": Interview with Charles Sehe, December 8, 2001, Admiral Nimitz Historic Site, Center for Pacific War Studies, Fredericksburg, VA, 2.

118 "The *West Virginia* was awash and burning, the *Oklahoma* had capsized, the *California* was listing and afire": Craig Nelson, *Pearl Harbor: From Infamy to Greatness* (New York: Scribner, 2016), 300.

119 "I felt a tremendous blow on my leg and looked down": Paul Joseph Travers, *Eyewitness to Infamy: An Oral History of Pearl Harbor, December 7, 1941* (Lanham, MD: Madison Books, 1991), 150.

121 "Wounded men, men without ships, men without clothing or shoes": Ibid., 157.

SOURCE NOTES

CHAPTER 13

126 "Do you think that the U.S. fleet will be able to operate out of Pearl Harbor within six months?": Craig Nelson, *Pearl Harbor: From Infamy to Greatness* (New York: Scribner, 2016), 311.

129 "December 7, 1941—*a date which will live in infamy*—the United States of America was suddenly and deliberately attacked by naval and air forces of the Empire of Japan": https://www.archives.gov/publications/prologue/2001/winter/crafting-day-of-infamy-speech.html.

CHAPTER 14

132 "Oh my God, that's my flag, my white handkerchief": Lawrence Rodriggs, *We Remember Pearl Harbor* (Newark, CA: Communications Concepts, 1991), 190.

133 "I was hiding behind my father, scared to death": Ibid., 191.

133 "If you guys don't trust us": Ibid.

135 "About a half-mile from the gate": Ibid., 27.

135 "This marine came up to me, he pointed the rifle right at me": Ibid.

136 "You, David Kobata, say you pledge your loyalty to the United States": Duncan Ryūken Williams, *American Sutra: A Story of Faith and Freedom in the Second World War* (Cambridge, MA: The Belknap Press of Harvard University Press, 2019), e-book location 816.

137 *"Oh, Kimi-chan, Kiho shinde kara, no,* Queen's Hospital *ni tsurete kitoruke"*: Oral history interview with Kimiko Watanabe, April 21, 1992, Waialua, Oahu, "An Era of Change: Oral Histories of Civilians in World War II Hawaii," Center for Oral History, University of Hawai'i at Mano'a, 1314.

139 "Nobody came": Ibid., 1317.

CHAPTER 15

141 "And then he was with us again": Stephen Bower Young, *Trapped at Pearl Harbor: Escape from Battleship* Oklahoma (Annapolis, MD: Naval Institute Press, 2013), 111.

SOURCE NOTES

142 "We could hear people pounding on the ship": Ibid., 135.

143 "They gave us clean, new, specially marked buckets": Interview with Charles Sehe, December 8, 2001, Admiral Nimitz Historic Site, Center for Pacific War Studies, Fredericksburg, VA, 4.

143 "I recall finding torn arms, legs, heads, and body torsos, and broken bones": Ibid., 5.

143 "I realized her face had become an ashen mask": Mary Ann Ramsey, "Only Yesteryear," U.S. Naval Institute, *Naval History*, Winter 1991, page 2.

144 "The world's going to change quickly": Ibid., 3.

146 "Can you stand a hole through the bulkhead? We'll drill a small one through.": Young, *Trapped at Pearl Harbor*, 137.

CHAPTER 16

151 The thunderous radio broadcast of the attack: Mitsuo Fuchida, *For That One Day: The Memoirs of Mitsuo Fuchida, Commander of the Attack on Pearl Harbor*, trans. Douglas T. Shinsato and Tadamori Urabe (self-published book by the translators, 2001), 108.

151 "Standing directly across from His Majesty": Ibid., 109.

153 "Every day in Japan brought news of victory": Ibid., 126.

154 "There can be no peace": Steven M. Gillon, *Pearl Harbor: FDR Leads the Nation into War* (New York: Basic Books, 2011), 179.

156 "I think the time has come when we should all get behind our country"; "I'm behind Mr. Roosevelt one hundred percent"; "We all are brothers. Let us remain brothers": All quotations from oral history interviews collected by Alan Lomax for the Library of Congress, "After the Day of Infamy: 'Man-on-the-Street' Interviews Following the Attack on Pearl Harbor," https://www.loc.gov/collections/interviews-following-the-attack-on-pearl-harbor/about-this-collection/.

158 "Strength gradually went out of me": Ensign Kazuo Sakamaki, *I Attacked Pearl Harbor: The True Story Told by the Midget Submarine Officer Who Became United States P.O.W. #1*, trans. Toru Matsumoto, ed. Gary R. Coover (Honolulu: Rollston Press, 2017), 92.

SOURCE NOTES

CHAPTER 17

163 "The way things are now, we have about enough to get us within 200 miles of the China coast, and that's all": James M. Scott, *Target Tokyo: Jimmy Doolittle and the Raid that Avenged Pearl Harbor* (New York: W. W. Norton, 2015), 178.

164 "If anyone wants to withdraw": Ibid.

164 "I was scared": Ibid.

166 "It was a beautiful spring day with not a cloud in the sky": Ibid., 226.

167 "I saw fifteen to twenty bodies which had fallen as if they were hit by our bombardier's fire": Ibid., 202.

EPILOGUE: PEARL HARBOR MEMORIES

174 "We lost it because of the war": Lawrence Rodriggs, *We Remember Pearl Harbor* (Newark, CA: Communications Concepts, 1991), 77.

176 "the first and probably saddest flight of my life": Mary Ann Ramsey, "Only Yesteryear," U.S. Naval Institute, *Naval History*, Winter 1991, 4.

180 "Tell everyone I couldn't have missed it for anything": Gwyneth Rhiannon Milbrath, "The Bombing of Pearl Harbor, Hawaii, December 7, 1941," chapter 6 of Arlene Keeling and Barbara Mann Wall, eds., *Nurses and Disasters: Global, Historical Case Studies* (New York: Springer, 2015), 162.

182 "He's still living in Tennessee": Interview with Charles Sehe, December 8, 2001, Admiral Nimitz Historic Site, Center for Pacific War Studies, Fredericksburg, VA, 4.

182 "All those men that were lost": Ibid.

FOR FURTHER READING

Hundreds of books have been written on the Pearl Harbor attacks. Here is a selection of the best, written from different perspectives and for different reading levels.

Allen, Thomas. *Remember Pearl Harbor: American and Japanese Survivors Tell Their Stories*. New York: National Geographic Kids, 2016.
A thorough narrative of December 7, 1941, with vivid photographs and other graphics.

Cook, Theodore, and Haruko Taya Cook. *Japan at War: An Oral History*. New York: New Press, 1992.
An oral history of the Pacific War from the Japanese perspective, including unique accounts of the Pearl Harbor attack as understood by Japan.

Cutrer, Thomas W., and T. Michael Parrish. *Doris Miller, Pearl Harbor, and the Birth of the Civil Rights Movement*. College Station: Texas A&M University Press, 2018.
A biography of the most famous African American sailor involved in the fight against the Japanese attack.

Dower, John W. *War Without Mercy: Race and Power in the Pacific War*. New York: Pantheon Books, 1987.
An in-depth look by a major scholar on the role that racism played in the Pacific War.

Gillon, Steven M. *Pearl Harbor: FDR Leads the Nation into War*. New York: Basic Books, 2011.
  The history of Pearl Harbor as seen through the eyes of President Roosevelt and his White House advisers.

LaForte, Robert S., and Ronald E. Marcello, eds. *Remembering Pearl Harbor: Eyewitness Accounts by U.S. Military Men and Women*. Wilmington, DE: SR Books, 1991.
  Comprehensive first-person interviews with military personnel who experienced the attacks directly.

Nelson, Craig. *Pearl Harbor: From Infamy to Greatness*. New York: Scribner, 2016.
  A nonfiction book that reads like a novel, presenting the history of the Pearl Harbor attacks from many different sides, bringing in the voices and perspectives of hundreds of participants.

Prange, Gordon. *At Dawn We Slept: The Untold Story of Pearl Harbor*. New York: Penguin Books, 1982.
  The classic account of the Pearl Harbor attack, written from an exclusively US perspective.

Reeves, Richard. *Infamy: The Shocking Story of Japanese American Internment in World War II*. New York: Picador, 2016.
  A clear and thorough history of the experience of Japanese Americans interned during the war.

Rodriggs, Lawrence. *We Remember Pearl Harbor*. Newark, CA: Communications Concepts, 1991.
  A wonderful collection of interviews with civilians of all backgrounds who witnessed the Pearl Harbor attack firsthand.

Takei, George. *They Called Us Enemy*. San Diego: Top Shelf Productions, 2016.
  The *Star Trek* actor and activist tells the true story of his family's internment during War World II in a beautiful graphic novel format.

FOR FURTHER READING

Terkel, Studs. *"The Good War": An Oral History of World War II.* New York: New Press, 1997.

A prizewinning oral history of the World War II experience, from many different perspectives, including how people first reacted to the news of Pearl Harbor.

Travers, Paul Joseph. *Eyewitness to Infamy: An Oral History of Pearl Harbor, December 7, 1941.* Lanham, MD: Madison Books, 1991.

First-person interviews with sailors, soldiers, and other military personnel who experienced the Pearl Harbor attacks.

Twomey, Steve. *Countdown to Pearl Harbor: The Twelve Days to the Attack.* New York: Simon & Schuster, 2016.

A day-by-day story of the twelve days leading up to the Pearl Harbor attacks, seen from many different perspectives all over the United States—offering a glimpse of life in America on the eve of World War II.

Wenger, J. Michael, Robert J. Cressman, and John F. Di Virgilio. *This Is No Drill: The History of NAS Pearl Harbor and the Japanese Attacks of 7 December 1941.* Annapolis, MD: Naval Institute Press, 2018.

For those wishing to go deeper into the history of the Pearl Harbor base itself, a richly detailed story of the military installation there and an account of the attacks based on government archives.

MULTIMEDIA RESOURCES

https://www.history.navy.mil/browse-by-topic/wars-conflicts-and -operations/world-war-ii/1941/pearl-harbor.html

Created by the US Navy, a heavily documented website with links to photographs, oral history, and detailed information about the different Navy ships attacked on December 7.

https://www.archives.gov/news/topics/remembering-pearl-harbor

An exhibit at the National Archives with links to different multimedia resources, including FDR's famous "Infamy" speech on December 8, 1941.

FOR FURTHER READING

https://www.loc.gov/rr/program/journey/pearlharbor.html
  Links to a rich array of online resources, including oral history interviews with survivors of the attack.

https://www.gilderlehrman.org/history-resources/online-exhibitions/attack-pearl-harbor-map-based-exhibition
  A detailed interactive map exhibit, describing the Pearl Harbor attack as it unfolded.

INDEX

Page numbers in *italics* refer to illustrations in the text.

INDEX

INDEX

MOLLY GLASGOW

MARC FAVREAU

is the director of editorial programs at
the New Press, the acclaimed author of
Crash and *Spies*, coauthor (with Michael
Eric Dyson) of *Unequal*, and coeditor
(with Ira Berlin and Steven F. Miller) of
*Remembering Slavery: African Americans
Talk About Their Personal Experiences of
Slavery and Emancipation*. He lives in
Martha's Vineyard, Massachusetts.